Little Eyes That See the Glory

Lead Your Children into Encountering God

Dana Bellamy

Little Eyes That See The Glory by Dana Bellamy
Published by Dana Bellamy
Copyright © 2022 Dana Bellamy

All rights reserved. No portion of this book may be reproduced in any form without permission from the publisher, except as permitted by U.S. copyright law.

Cover Designed by Kiera Bellamy

Print ISBN: 979-8-9866871-0-0
Ebook ISBN: 979-8-9866871-2-4

Printed in the United States of America
First Edition

Scripture taken from the New King James Version®. Copyright © 1982 by Thomas Nelson. Used by permission. All rights reserved.

Contents

Introduction 1
Chapter 1 - It is the Goodness of God 3
Chapter 2 - The Spirit of Fear 17
Chapter 3 - Consent and Cooperation 27
Chapter 4 - Powerful Spiritual Truths 45
Chapter 5 - Seek God for His Direction
    for Your Children 63
Chapter 6 - Seek God for the Big
    and the Little Things 77
Chapter 7 - Practical Ways to Encourage
    Children to Know the Lord 87
Chapter 8 - Encourage Your Kids to
    Spend Time With The Lord 101
Chapter 9 - Light a Fire in the Hearts
    of Your Children 107
Chapter 10 - My Children's Testimonies 113
About the Author 121

Introduction

We, as parents, are called to make disciples of our children. It is our privilege and duty to steward our children's hearts and do the most significant and powerful thing we can do for them - Introduce them to Jesus and equip them to cultivate an intimate relationship with Him.

Other parents have different priorities when it comes to raising their children. For example, they teach their baby to read while they are still in diapers. They put their children in many extra-curricular activities such as sports and dance. They facilitate their children's education so that they can go to a good college, have a career, and therefore be successful in the world. While there is nothing wrong with that in and of itself, we have to keep the main thing the main thing.

The Bible says in Mark 8:36-37, "For what will it profit a man if he gains the whole world, and loses his own soul? Or what will a man give in exchange for his soul?"

Nothing is more important for a parent to do than make sure that their children know Jesus! I am sure that you are reading this book because you already know this.

In this book, I will share the things that the Lord has taught me about raising my children to know Him and encounter

Him. I will also give guidance on dealing with issues that come up, such as fear, nightmares, and imaginary friends.

I am not going to sugar-coat and dance around truths. I want to help you and your children, so I will be open, honest, straightforward, and practical. The enemy has no problem attacking your kids. He's ruthless! I will make sure that you know how to keep your kids safe from all the schemes of the enemy, and, best of all, help them know Jesus intimately.

I will begin this book by guiding you through many of the enemy's traps, and then I will conclude by teaching you how to lead your children into a vibrant relationship with the Lord. I will share many beautiful testimonies of my own children's experiences with the Lord. You will also see that even though I have not experienced all of these things myself, the Lord has helped me to guide my children regardless. I will not hold them back from going further and deeper into the things of God than I have experienced myself. My ceiling will be their floor.

Chapter 1
It is the Goodness of God

The most powerful thing about children is that it is easier for them to be in tune with the Spirit of God than it is for the average adult. The reason for this is that they are not as conditioned by the ways of this world. They are not cynical and don't conform to the way this world works. They are fresh. They just believe.

We need to take advantage of this. Instead of letting our children become adults with callused hearts who are not in tune with the things of the Spirit, we can cultivate this advantage that they have. We can begin to teach them that partnering with the Holy Spirit is normal.

The spirit realm, where the Holy Spirit resides, is the *primary* realm. Some people think that the spirit realm is 'spooky' or that it is best to ignore it completely. However, the spirit realm existed before anything was created in this physical realm. In the fullness of time, God, who has always resided in the spirit realm, decided to create a physical world with physical laws such as time, space, and gravity, to have a place to put His children on.

Hebrews 11:3 says, "By faith we understand that the worlds were framed by the word of God, so that *the things which are seen were not made of things which are visible."* (Emphasis mine.)

In this Scripture, we can see that the things which we now see with our eyes, were made of things that are not visible. Therefore, the natural world was made *from* the spirit realm. We see this in the first chapter of Genesis.

Therefore, it is not good to teach our children to ignore the things they see and hear that originate from the spirit realm. Those things are even more real than this physical world. We need to encourage our kids that they are hearing from God, that God is speaking to them, and that they can see Him. Likewise, we need to equip them to know their position and authority in Christ so they can rebuke the enemy, the enemy's plans, and the lies he speaks to them.

The enemy doesn't take it easy on our kids because they're only kids. He is ruthless. We are our children's covering, and it is our mandate to teach these things to our children as they grow and can begin to understand.

Cultivating our children's hearts to be in tune with the Holy Spirit is vital to their success in life and throughout eternity. The more we can teach our children to be sensitive and obedient to the Holy Spirit's leading, the more they will accomplish for the Kingdom of God, and the more they will fulfill their destinies.

It Begins with You

So, how do we lead our children to love Jesus and be sensitive to the Holy Spirit? Very simply - it all begins with *you*.

When you begin by pursuing God with your whole heart, your relationship with God will flow out from you and profoundly impact your children. When you experience Jesus for yourself and walk in obedience to Him and to His Word, you will model the Christian walk in front of them. This is not a, 'do as I say but not as I do' process. Some of the staunchest atheists were once raised in 'Christian' homes. I say 'Christian' in quotes because they were Christian in word only and not in practice. The children in these homes might have experienced religion and witnessed their parents worshiping a God with seemingly no power in everyday life, not relevant for today, and full of judgment - misunderstanding God's true nature. Or perhaps they saw hypocrisy in their parents' lives which spoke a lot louder than their words. They could have even had parents that professed Christianity but weren't loving parents. Religion or hypocrisy like this can lead children to say in their hearts, "If that is what God is like, I don't want Him."

It is not good for a child's heart to see their parents profess one thing and then witness them do another. That's why our own walk with God is so important. When we passionately pursue Jesus with our whole hearts, we will close the door to religion and hypocrisy. When we model the *goodness* of God in front of our children and show them that God is a good and loving God Who loves them unconditionally and wants to be close to them, they will say, "I want what my parents have."

I know a man named *Mark who was violent. It seemed that he couldn't even go and get a meal at a fast-food restaurant without getting into some sort of altercation. This man's father was extremely violent. Mark told me a story once of a time his family went on an outing to the beach. While they were in the water together, Mark's father started to beat him. His father held him under the water so long that Mark thought he would drown. This experience, along with many others, affected him to the point where he was so hurt that he, too, became violent. Years later, Mark received salvation. His father-in-law, who was a good and loving father to his wife, led him to the Lord. During his early Christian walk, Mark still had a picture in his mind that God was like his earthly father. It was hindering his walk with God. One day God said to him, "Mark, I am not at all like your earthly father. I am more like your mother." Mark had a kind and loving mother. When Mark heard this, he was finally able to understand the true nature of God. I am happy to report that Mark and his wife are now in full-time ministry and passionate about the Lord. They are also raising two happy and godly children together.

As for myself, I grew up with a devoted and loving father. He never gave me a moment of grief, and I knew that he loved me unconditionally. Because of this, I am able to relate to my Heavenly Father according to His true nature. It was easy for me due to the example of my earthly father. I had an advantage that Mark didn't have. I was easily able to accept that God was a good Father to me, and my relationship with the Lord has always been effortless because of it.

The Bible declares in Romans 2:4 that it is the *goodness* of God that leads us to repentance.

It is the *goodness*. It's not the guilt, fear, or condemnation. When we show our children how *good* God is towards us, they will never run to the enemy and his stuff. Nor will they hesitate to run right back to God's arms when they mess up. They won't be afraid of Him.

It is dangerous and counter-productive to make your kids afraid of God's judgment or of hell. If your kids are scared of God or afraid of going to hell, they may choose to turn to God, but only reluctantly and out of obligation. It will never be genuine and heartfelt repentance - repentance means 'to change one's mind'. Scaring your children like this could be compared to giving them an option to eat either a spider or a brussels sprout. Sure, they will eat the brussels sprout over the spider, but that doesn't mean that they *like* the brussels sprout or would continue to choose the brussels sprout even if something else came along.

When people realize that comparatively, God is an all-you-can-eat buffet created by the top Michelin-starred chefs in the world, they would immediately run to Him to partake!

Through our continued pursuit of God and the resultant overflow our children receive from our vibrant relationship with God, they will learn to run to Him.

My Story

When I was a child growing up in Australia, my parents weren't religious at all. They also weren't church-goers. Yet, they did tell us that God is a loving God and showed us how to pray to Him. They also told us that there were angels around us, protecting us. My dad would come into our rooms at night - I had three sisters and a brother, and I was the second eldest- and he would pray with us. It was a rote prayer that we would say together in the German language. (My parents were German, and I was born in Germany. We all moved to Australia when I was just over a year old). The rote prayer was a German lullaby. It was a prayer for God to watch over us as we slept.

When I got older, I would repeat this prayer on my own every night before bed. And looking back, I can see how the Lord took me by the hand and guided me into a closer relationship with Him. I will share more stories throughout this book. I will also share stories from my children, which blow my stories out of the water. My kids are truly standing on my shoulders. My ceiling is their floor. That's the way it should be.

So, one day I mentioned to my auntie, Karin, that I pray every night. She said to me, "You need to *mean* what you pray." It came across as a bit of a rebuke, but she was right. I had to *mean* what I prayed. So, that gave me a course correction, and from then on, I didn't pray on auto-pilot with my mind elsewhere. I was present in my mind with the Lord as I prayed every night. This was a step forward in my relationship with Him.

I feel led to continue my testimony on how I remained a Believer in Christ my whole life and never have, and never will, turn my back on God. I now know that God was speaking to me my whole life, although I didn't know it at the time. I only realized that I could hear His voice after I was married and already had two of my six kids!

One day as an adult, I was thinking about God. I was thinking about how God is Omnipresent, Omnipotent, and Omniscient

- All-Present, All-Powerful, and All-Knowing. But more than that, I realized that no one had ever taught me that. I just knew in my heart that it was the truth. So I asked the Lord about this, and He replied, "It's because *I* told you." Wow! That blew me away. I am sure that this is also true for you.

Romans 1:18-20 confirms this: "For the wrath of God is revealed from heaven against all ungodliness and unrighteousness of men, who suppress the truth in unrighteousness, *because what may be known of God is manifest in them, for God has shown it to them.* For since the creation of the world His invisible *attributes* are clearly seen, being understood by the things that are made, *even* His eternal power and Godhead, so that they are without excuse." (Emphasis mine).

It is such a powerful truth that God has already revealed Himself and His invisible attributes to us and our children. They already have an inner knowing that God is their Heavenly Father. God also reveals Himself to our children through His creation which speaks very clearly that there is a Creator.

Trusting God

Another time, I remember God developing trust in my heart towards Him. I had done something naughty one day, just being a kid. But I knew that my mom would not let it slide; She would surely punish me for it. I quickly prayed to God, and a miracle happened. I got no punishment whatsoever. I got off scot-free.

A while later, I was playing with my siblings at the front of my home. The Lord reminded me that I had prayed about that situation, and He had heard my cry and answered my prayer. I didn't realize at the time that it was God Who spoke to my heart. I just thought that I had randomly remembered. But I realized that He had answered my prayer, and I *knew* that it would have *had* to have been an act of God. And so, I praised Him and thanked Him for it. (I was usually a good kid, trust me.)

Another time I was having a hard time with a bully at school. She was tough and scary to me. One day I was waiting at the bus stop at the front of my High School - High School is from 7th to 12th grades in Australia, and I was in one of the lower grades - and I got wind of the fact that she was going to come to where I was and have a physical confrontation with me. I was afraid, and I prayed fervently to God. She never came, and I was thankful to God. I acknowledged Him once again for answering my prayer.

He also answered it further. I was friends with a girl who was kind but also tough. We were in the same dance school together, and we were often paired up to perform duo's together - which were dances with just the two of us. She came from a family of Boxers. She knew how to fight, and everybody knew it. One afternoon I came to one of our weekly dance lessons looking forlorn. She asked me what was wrong. I knew that she didn't like people complaining to her and wanting her to stick up for them, so I hadn't said anything. But since she asked me, I let her know what was happening with this bully. My friend started smiling. She said that that bully really sucks up to her and that she would deal with it at school tomorrow. It was a load off my mind. The next afternoon, I was sitting by myself on the pavement outside of the town library, up the road from our High School. The bully saw me and came and squatted down in front of me. I was taken aback, and I didn't know what to expect. I then quickly noticed that her demeanor wasn't harsh and confrontational. She surprisingly looked a little sheepish. She then proceeded to let me know that my friend had come and talked with her and that she was afraid that now she had an enemy in my friend, and she didn't want that. She asked for my forgiveness, and I gave it to her. That was the last of the bullying. Go, God!!

When you have experiences like this growing up, it makes it easy to trust God. This is because He shows Himself to be strong over and over again. When we start teaching our kids that God really is an 'ever-present help in time of need' and teach them to pray and expect answers, they will have their own experiences and develop their own trust-relationship with Him. They will see for themselves that not only is God real, but also that He cares about them and even the things that they care about. Psalms 46:1 KJV confirms that "God *is* our refuge and strength, a very present help in trouble."

My relationship with God wasn't intimate yet. I knew God was God, I loved Him, I had begun to trust Him, but I still saw Him as a far-away God Who wasn't Someone that was involved in my everyday life.

God Really Cares

I finished 12th grade and took the final exams for all my subjects. I then waited for my score to be posted, ranking me amongst all the 12th-grade students of the whole Australian state of New South Wales. (New South Wales is the most populated state in Australia. I lived on the outskirts of Sydney.) I called the phone number to hear my score. I was expecting to hear the number 70. That meant that I basically performed better than 69% of the state. (To get a score of 100 meant that you performed the best in the state.) I hadn't really tried very hard or studied very much, but I figured that I would do well enough to get a score of 70. My plan was to become a fighter pilot in the Royal Australian Air Force. So, I waited on the phone to hear the number.

I heard 53.65. I was devastated. That was not even close to good enough! I felt defeated. It was a wake-up call. I remember sitting in my living room, probably looking like a sad sack of potatoes, letting my parents know about the news. My dad spoke something to me that I have never forgotten, even over twenty years later. He spoke an oracle from God, even though I didn't fully realize it at the time. It not only changed the course of my life but also my relationship with God. He said, "Dana, your heartfelt desire comes from God, and just know that He will show you the way." I thought, "Wow. Does God really care about me *that much*? Does he really care about what I care about? Is this desire really bigger than me?"

The statement really hit my heart, and it endeared me to God. I wanted to know Him more if He was *that* good!

I just wanted to take a moment from this story and interject something here. I have only recently fully realized that that statement made by my dad was the turning point in my life. It was then that I started to understand how good God was, and it was then that I really started pursuing Him with my whole heart. This was a perfect picture of Romans 2:4 in my life. It was only when I realized how *good* God was that I ran towards Him with all my heart. And it has been over two decades since that day, and I am *still* in awe of God's goodness as He keeps revealing Himself to me. I just wanted to point out that my parents were not religious at all. I never grew up thinking that God was a hard taskmaster and that nothing I did really pleased Him. My parents simply told me that God loved me and simple truths like that. I hope you can see how impactful my father's words were to me and to the course of my life. Had he not chosen to be sensitive to the Holy Spirit in that moment and speak to me what the Lord was saying to me, I wouldn't have run to God at that time.

Continuing with my story, I ended up deciding to go back to High School and complete grades eleven and twelve again to get the score that I needed to be able to pursue my dream. I will spare you the details, but God supernaturally led us to enroll me in a Christian Private School called 'Broughton Anglican College'. Upon enrolling, I was given a journal (that every student receives to record homework, etc.) and a Bible. I was so happy to have my own Bible. I decided that I would read the Bible and start pressing into God. I was so new to the Bible I didn't even know that it was made up of smaller books or that there was an Old and New Testament! I started getting familiar with it as I read and also through the daily Bible Studies that were conducted every morning at the school.

The Lord connected me with a friend who also loved the Lord. She would show me things in the Bible that were fascinating to me. She showed me in the Bible that it was important to get baptized - by full immersion in water, not a 'sprinkling on the head' as a baby - and to be filled with the Holy Spirit with the evidence of speaking in tongues, which she told me was a 'secret prayer language.' I thought, "Ooh, a *secret prayer language*. How mysterious." I wanted it. I went to her church with her and got baptized in a bathtub in front of the whole congregation of about 200 people. I was the only one. When I was raised back up out of the water but still sitting in the bathtub, the pastor was praying for me to receive the Baptism of the Holy Spirit. He then prayed over me and helped me to start speaking in tongues myself. I was elated as I spoke out in that secret prayer language!

I continued to press into God after that, not always perfectly. But my *heart* was perfect towards Him. I finished school and received a score of 86.80! That was cool to have such a turn-around. I then applied to become a fighter pilot in the Royal Australian Air Force. I even got to the last selection phase where I was flown across the state and flew with ex-fighter pilots to test my flying ability and retention skills. There was tough competition, and ultimately, I wasn't selected to continue. Looking back now, I see that I didn't have the grace to continue with that. That was not God's best for me, but God used the whole experience of returning to school and preparing for the Air Force for my good. Even now, when I am homeschooling my kids, I can understand math really well. Who'd have thought? Also, I know that the Lord is not finished with His promise to me regarding aviation. Last year, the Lord led my husband and me to purchase an airplane and open a Flight School called 'On The Fly Aviation' here in Texas. I got back on my pilot journey and have recently received my Pilot's License! God is so faithful.

I am looking forward to everything else He has planned for us in the field of aviation.

A Divine Appointment

During that time when I went back to school, I had an on-again-off-again boyfriend who was not a Believer. Upon counsel from my then Pastor, I broke it off with him. I determined in my heart that I would wait as long as it takes, but I will only marry the one God has for me. I wanted to be equally yoked with a strong Believer and raise my kids to love the Lord.

The Lord was faithful. The Lord brought my husband, Will, to Sydney, Australia, from the United States via Iraq. He was a United States Marine returning from the war in Iraq and pulled into port on the USS Pearl Harbor for a 'Rest and Recreation' stop in Sydney. Through a word God spoke to me, He made sure I was out in Darling Harbour, Sydney, that night, and it was supernatural how we met. If you're interested, I have the whole story chronicled in my first book, Raising Happy Hearts.

I married Will and moved to the United States to live with him. We lived on Camp Pendleton in California. I had only been there a couple of months when Will's uncle offered to fly me to Tulsa, Oklahoma, to join him and Will's parents at a conference at their church. I agreed. This would be the first time I had met Will's parents. I should also mention that there was something on my mind. My husband's Marine Unit was gearing up to return to Iraq for their second deployment, and he was just about to leave me for seven weeks of training. This was devastating for me at the time. I was new to the country and hardly knew anyone at all. I didn't know how I would fare if he left.

I flew to Tulsa to meet Will's parents. Will's dad was getting a degree from Oral Roberts University at the time. We went to the conference that Dave Roberson hosted at his church. Dave Roberson has spent many, many years pressing into God, and he has written a powerful book about the power of praying in tongues, which I highly recommend, called, 'The Walk of the Spirit, The Walk of Power.' During the conference, I started seeing miracles. I saw a lady's arm move and become the same length as her other arm as the Lord healed her back. Another lady was healed of Diabetes.

A Touch from God

I stood in the prayer line and waited to get my own touch from the Spirit. Dave Roberson came to me and laid his hands on both sides of my neck so gently. He said, "And you little one…" and then I fell out in the Spirit. After a short while, I got up to go back to my chair. I wrote those words in my book to keep a record of what was said to me. Will's uncle came and sat next to me and saw what I had written. He told me that unbeknownst to me, he was a 'catcher' who stood behind the lines of people to catch them as they fell. He was right next to me when Dave Roberson spoke to me. He told me that what I had written down was not all that Dave had said to me. Will's uncle informed me that his full statement was, "And you little one, you don't even know what is growing inside you."

Wow. It turns out that I was just a *few days* pregnant with my firstborn, Kiera. That was amazing! However, I still had the worry in my mind about Will's seven-week training. I stood in another prayer line when another preacher was praying. He went down the line and prayed for people. Everyone was falling out under the power of God. I fell out too. But I got right back up because I didn't get my answer. The preacher saw me on his way back to the stage, pointed at me, and firmly said, "You have such a sweet heart, and God would move Heaven and Earth for you!" Something hit me at that moment. I know now that I simultaneously received a touch from the Lord. I burst out crying, no, *sobbing* into my hands. God *loved* me. *God* loved me. God loved *me!* Right then and there, I received a supernatural revelation of His love.

Then, when I read the Bible and saw the *same* passages that speak about God loving the world, I was able to take it personally. Yes, he loves everyone, but He loves *me*. I finally had a *revelation* of it. And I pray right now that if you haven't received a revelation of His love, that you will right *now*, in Jesus' precious name!

If you were wondering, my husband ended up going to that seven-week-long training. Yet, he got so much favor with his command, and the Lord gave him many opportunities to come back and visit me throughout the seven-week timespan. The Lord even sent me ladies from the church we had just started attending. They watched over me and took me to church events and even out to eat. He is such a good Father.

God is Nearby

So, that was just a taste of how God wooed me into a more intimate relationship with Him. I have continued to mature in the Lord and dive deeper and deeper into knowing and experiencing Him.

I want to share one more testimony about what the Lord used to show me that He was way closer than I realized. I was on the phone with one of Will's sisters early on in my marriage with Will. His sister has an amazing relationship with the Lord and is really prophetic. She was telling me about something and then she couldn't remember the details of what she was about to say. It was then that she did something that just blew me away. She said to me, "Hold on a sec." She paused, and I heard her say, "What was it again, God? Oh yeah…" and then got back on the line with the answer. She asked the Lord for the answer, just like we would ask our family members a question. She waited for the reply, not doubting her ability to hear, and then got right back on the line with the answer, like it was the most natural thing in the world. What?!?!?

Through that small incident and other such conversations with Will's sister, I realized that God was indeed as close to me as the air between my fingertips. He wasn't a far-away God. We need to have that revelation for ourselves and instill this knowledge into our children. This is what God desires for all His children: To be in constant fellowship with Him. He has wanted this fellowship since the beginning. It's exactly what He had intended before the fall of man. 1 Thessalonians 5:16-18 says, "Rejoice always, *pray without ceasing*, in everything give thanks; for this is the will of God in Christ Jesus for you." (Emphasis, mine) Prayer is a two-way conversation. God wants us to maintain a conversation with Him throughout the day and night. He wants to be our primary focus. I will talk more about this later on in this book.

As you can see through my testimony, God pursued me, and I responded. We can partner with Him to help draw our kids into having a close and intimate relationship with Him, but the pressure is not on us. We can relax and trust God to draw our kids to Himself. The Bible says, in John 6:44, "No one can come to Me unless the Father who sent Me draws him; and I will raise him up at the last day." Jesus also said in John 15:4, "I am the vine, you *are* the branches. He who abides in Me, and I in him, bears much fruit; for without Me you can do nothing."

The main thing for us, as parents, to do is to pursue God and yield to Him in everything, including in raising our children. We are not alone in this. We can't do anything without Him, but when we yield to Him, we will bear much fruit, and so will our children. God will help us to raise them in a way that makes it easy for them to know that He is good and to receive Him as Lord and Savior of their lives. We can rest in that.

You can also see that God had a lot of work to do in my life to teach me about Himself and His Word. It took a lot of time. But now, my children will not have to start where I started. My ceiling is my children's floor. I effortlessly pour wisdom and instruction into my children. They eat of the fruit of my relationship with God. They are *already* having experiences with the Lord that I still dream of having!

It is the same for you, too. Your ceiling is your children's floor. The higher you go in the Lord and the closer you are in your relationship with Him, the greater head-start your children will have in their walks with the Lord. This is why the most powerful thing that you can do for your children is to press into God for yourself and allow the fruit of your relationship with God to flow over into them. It will flow through your instruction, example, and sharing regular testimonies of God showing up in your life.

Chapter 2
The Spirit of Fear

We all deal with fear during different seasons of our lives, and for different reasons. Our kids can also deal with fear. Kids can see into the spirit realm more easily than adults can because they are not hindered in their spiritual sight like most of us are. They often can see things that we, as adults, cannot see. In this chapter, I will share what I have learned about how to completely get rid of fear. I will also help you teach your kids to stay free from the sources of fear so you can have a peaceful home.

I will begin by sharing my testimony on how I learned to be free from the Spirit of fear, my children's testimonies, and how I have taught them to be free.

When I felt fear as a kid, I just felt fear. I didn't know anything about the spiritual realm, other than about God and His angels - and if there were demons, they certainly weren't anywhere near me! Therefore, I didn't know *how* to combat the fear or even that I *could* combat it. One thing I did learn on my own was that if I watched something scary before bed, I went to bed scared of everything. However, if I watched something wholesome, I went to bed without a care in the world. I decided for myself that I was going to be careful about what I watched, and I stopped watching anything that was scary to me.

A Wakeup Call

When I married my husband, I moved halfway across the world from Sydney, Australia, to Camp Pendleton, California. I didn't know anyone there except my husband and a few of his work buddies, and I thought it was the perfect time to focus more on God and get closer to Him. I wasn't legally allowed to work in the United States yet, so I spent the majority of my time at home by myself. Our home on the Marine Corps Base was newly renovated right before we moved in. The people who stayed in the home before we did trashed the place, and that's why it had to be completely renovated before we moved in. During this time, I was too shy to even pray out loud in front of Will. I wasn't confident in my praying ability. I was new to the deeper things of God and a new wife all at the same time.

One day, while my husband was at work, I decided to worship the Lord. I didn't want him to catch me in the 'act of worship' because I was shy about it, and I was never sure when he would return home. The US Marines don't just work 9-5 every weekday. So, Will would come home after PT (Physical Training) in the mornings and sometimes at lunch, and I didn't know when to expect him. As I was worshiping in our living room, I was standing in front of a large old-school CD-Player on the floor in front of me. It was about one foot high and had a flat top where a stack of about six CDs was piled. I had worship music playing, and I was standing about two feet in front of it, facing it, with my eyes closed and my hands raised in worship. Every now and again I would hear a sound by my front door, which was behind me and to my right. I was fearful that Will was going to walk in on me worshiping, and I would've been so embarrassed about that. So, every time I would hear a noise, I would stop worshiping and run to the door to look out the window to see if Will had arrived. When I saw that he wasn't there, I would go back to worship.

After I had been worshiping for a while, something really strange happened. The stack of six CDs sitting on top of the CD-Player flew forward through the air and landed at my feet.

I looked down at them in shock. I thought to myself, "That did *not* just happen!" There was no way in the natural world that that could've happened. Science wouldn't have been able to explain that. I stood there in shock for a while, but then I had to make a decision. So I thought to myself, "I can either get *really* scared right now, or I can just keep worshiping God." To my credit, I decided to worship God.

Later that evening, I told Will about what had happened with the CDs as we went for a walk together in the neighborhood. He wasn't surprised at all. He was familiar with the supernatural. He replied nonchalantly, "Yeah, that was probably a demon." He then proceeded to tell me all about his, and his family's, past supernatural experiences, and not the angelic kind either. He told me about all the demonic manifestations they had experienced over the years! It was too much for my mind to handle. It put me into even more fear! He realized later that it wasn't wise to tell me all that right then, but the damage had already been done.

We got home, and soon it was time to go to bed. We were going to be intimate, but I told Will that I couldn't do it because I felt like we were being watched. We turned off the light and crawled into bed, which was an air mattress on the floor. Unfortunately, our furniture hadn't arrived on the moving truck yet, so we didn't have any furniture in the house. I was facing the wall, and Will was behind me, cuddled up to me. We spoke for a little while, and Will kept saying that he was hearing things in the home, such as plates being broken. I couldn't hear what he was hearing, but his comments were putting me into even more fear. I had moved beyond fear and was now completely petrified. I couldn't think of any thoughts that *weren't* fearful. The fear was all over me.

In the darkness, I heard Will call my name - he later told me that he called my name because he felt my heart beating super fast as he lay close to me. When I heard him call my name, I realized that I had my eyes wide open and was staring at the wall in front of me even though the room was completely dark. I hadn't realized that my eyes were even open before then.

Will then said, "Turn around and face towards me." As I turned around, I heard the large box of Gobstoppers, which was sitting on the floor beside the bed, tip over. I didn't think anything of it until I saw Will, with his head lifted off his pillow, staring at it. My heart started to beat faster. I nervously asked Will, "Did you knock them over?" He replied quickly, "Don't worry about it. Go to sleep." I pleaded with him, "*Please* tell me that you knocked them over." He once again answered, "Don't worry about it. Go to sleep."

A strong emotion consumed me at that moment, and it definitely wasn't the urge to sleep. I thought I was completely petrified before, but now I was even more so!!

A Turning Point

Will offered to go into the living room and turn on some worship music. I agreed. As he left the room, he turned on the bedroom light. I was able to see that the Gobstoppers were too far away from the bed for Will to even reach. He definitely couldn't have been the one who knocked them over. He called me into the living room, and we stood together in an embrace as the worship music played. Will was looking into my eyes as he prayed in tongues. I was still consumed with fear at that point. I had even become afraid of Will! I was looking into his eyes as he prayed in tongues and thought to myself, "If his eyes change, I am running out that door and down the street!" Right then, Will calmly spoke these words, "Spirit of fear, I command you to leave in Jesus' name."

Immediately all the fear left, and I was in complete peace. We sat on the carpet together in front of the CD player that was still playing worship music. So many thoughts were going through my head; I marveled at how I could be so completely consumed by fear one minute and the next minute, be entirely at peace. A minute earlier, I couldn't think of *anything* that didn't bring me great fear, and the next minute, I could objectively look at all that just happened as if I were a bystander. I saw the absolute and immediate power of the name of Jesus. Will didn't even yell the name of Jesus - he just knew his authority and simply and calmly *spoke* the name of Jesus in faith. And wow! Such power was released!!

I also marveled at the stark realization that the spirit realm was a lot closer than I had always thought. I thought that God was so far away, and I also thought that the enemy, and his demons, were so far away. I was now starting to realize that I was very wrong.

A few days later, Will had to go on an extended training exercise because he was getting ready to be deployed back to Iraq. He left for ten days. I was now completely alone and had to use my newly found revelation of the authority I had in the name of Jesus Christ to cast out demons. It felt daunting, but I thought to myself, "Right! I know what to do! If a demon comes back, I will just tell it to go in Jesus' name, just as Will had done."

When I went to sleep at night, I was always trying to sleep with one eye open, just in case a demon *dared* to come back! I realized that this wasn't a good method. It is impossible to be on the lookout for demons and get to sleep at the same time. Also, instead of just going on with my life and giving all my thoughts and focus to Jesus, all of my thoughts were consumed with looking out for demons so that I can deal with them if they came back. Therefore, I wasn't in my peace anymore. I wasn't petrified like I was that one night, but I definitely wasn't in peace.

When I tried to sleep in this way, I noticed that I would wake up every hour throughout the night. I definitely wasn't sleeping peacefully.

The Victory

Then the Lord reminded me of an important lesson I had learned in my childhood. When I had peaceful thoughts, I was at peace in my bed. When I had fearful thoughts, I was fearful in my bed. He reminded me of Philippians 4:8 "Finally, brethren, whatever things are true, whatever things *are* noble, whatever things *are* just, whatever things *are* pure, whatever things *are* lovely, whatever things *are* of good report, if *there is* any virtue and if *there is* anything praiseworthy—meditate on these things."

He also highlighted Isaiah 26:3, which will always be one of my very favorite verses. It is also a powerful Scripture that confirms this truth. Isaiah 26:3 reads, "You will keep *him* in perfect peace, *Whose* mind *is* stayed *on You,* Because he trusts in You."

The Lord showed me that I don't gain victory over the enemy by giving him all my attention and waiting for him to show up. All that does is give the enemy all the power. I was still in a level of fear because I had my mind *stayed* on the enemy. But, when I decided to purposefully shift my attention from focusing on the enemy to focusing on God, His goodness, and the things that always made me happy (such as thinking about all the good times I had with my family back in Australia) I stayed in my peace, and I slept through the night.

I realized that the enemy only had power over me if I gave it to him by thinking about him or agreeing with the thoughts he was planting in my mind. As long as I didn't think about him, or things that were scary to me, he had no power over me. I stayed out of fear, and there were no more manifestations. (To be clear, all the manifestations stopped after Will took his authority the first time. They never started up again.)

Therefore, it is important that we, as parents, use the authority we have in the name of Jesus and don't allow the enemy into our homes. We also need to teach our kids the truth about how powerful our thoughts and what we choose to focus on are. Whatever we focus on, we magnify. If we focus on the enemy, we allow the enemy to become magnified in our lives. But when we focus on Jesus, the enemy loses all his power against us.

More Revelation

I want to share something else that has also helped me when fear tried to grip me, and I wasn't careful with my thoughts.

Will and I moved back to Australia in 2005, and we were temporarily living with my parents during that time. I started to notice that certain manifestations of the enemy had begun to happen around the house. It wasn't my house, so we took authority over the room we were staying in. But instead of doing what 2 Corinthians 10:5 says: "Casting down arguments and every high thing that exalts itself against the knowledge of God, *bringing every thought into captivity to the obedience of Christ,*" (emphasis mine), I kept thinking about what had been happening. Thus, I gave an inroad to the enemy and was in fear again as I lay on my bed that night. I realized that I was in fear, and so I spoke out 2 Timothy 1:7 quietly under my breath, "For God has not given us a spirit of fear, but of power and of love and of a sound mind." I noticed that after I had repeated it twice under my breath, all those fearful thoughts left me, and I was in my peace again.

So, this is another powerful key. The Word of God is the 'Sword of the Spirit.' It is a weapon against the enemy. All I did was quote the Scripture in a *whisper*, and the fear completely left.

Another night, many years later, I was lying in my bed, and I started to see visions of demonic-looking black images in my imagination. I was taught that when images randomly pop up in your imagination (or your mind's eye), those things are not *just* in your imagination. They are actually beings right there in front of you in the spirit. You are not seeing them with your natural eyes, but your spiritual eyes are seeing them. It is easy to blow it off and think that what you are looking at is *just your imagination* when in reality, it's not just your imagination at all! So, when I realized what I was seeing and paid attention to what it was, I opened my mouth and commanded them to go in Jesus' name! Immediately, I saw a shield come up and a sword come down. I was shocked and amazed! When the shield and sword left my vision, the black images were gone. I thought to myself, "Wow! The sword of the spirit and the shield of faith are real things!!" I hope that that is an encouragement to you. To clarify, I saw the sword and the shield in my imagination, but I know that it was not something that I had conjured up in my imagination because I certainly wasn't expecting to see that!

Another fear that I had to deal with was a lie I was believing. I spoke to a lady while I was at the conference in Tulsa, Oklahoma. This was the same conference that I had mentioned in the last chapter. She was a powerful intercessor. If you don't know what that means, it means that she was used powerfully by God to pray and intercede for other people. It goes without saying that she was a threat to the enemy and his plans. During one of our conversations, she told me that one day, satan himself walked into her bedroom in an effort to scare her into not praying anymore. (I used lower case on purpose for his name).

Because of this, I always believed that one day, when I was more of a threat to the enemy in my ministry, he would also come into my bedroom at night. To my credit, I didn't let it stop me, but it did still cause me a lot of fear. That fear was crushed through a teaching by Andrew Wommack. He is the President and Founder of Charis Bible College. This is the Bible College that Will and I both attended in Colorado, United States.

Before we attended the Bible college, I heard one of Andrew's teachings called "The Believer's Authority," and I highly recommend listening to it. You can listen to it for free on his website www.awmi.net. In this teaching, Andrew gives a story about the manifestations of the enemy that he has experienced and how he came to the revelation that the enemy can't do anything to you without your consent and cooperation. Once Andrew stopped believing that the enemy could manifest around him, the enemy no longer could. It was a powerful testimony for me to listen to. It showed me that even when I am a huge threat to the enemy like Andrew Wommack is, he *still* can't manifest himself to me. Hallelujah!

I realized that, in the past, when the enemy had manifested in my house, it was because I gave him my consent and cooperation by coming into agreement with the fearful thoughts he was giving to me. I didn't stand against them and cast them down as I do now. I also didn't know my authority and who I was in Christ. But when you know who you are in Christ, you are dangerous to the enemy.

As we grow in this truth in our lives, we will teach our children by our word and example, and they will not get pushed around by the enemy. Instead, they will stand up and take their authority and be dangerous to the kingdom of darkness.

A Friend's Testimony

I have a friend who has dealt with fear ever since she was a child and has only just received freedom from that fear as an adult. Here is her story in her own words:

Since I can remember, I was always afraid of everything, especially at night. I would lay awake at night listening for anything and everything for hours, petrified to move or even breathe! I certainly wasn't falling asleep. Into my adulthood, this fear never really left me - it just kind of morphed into other types of fear. I constantly had thoughts such as: What if something tragic happened to our family? What if someone got sick, hurt, or worse, died!? I always tried to stay one step ahead of the danger, which is exhausting and impossible when you're thinking in 'what ifs.'

Well, wouldn't you know it? Despite all my planning and thinking ahead, the enemy used this fear to gain access to our home regardless. My six-year-old daughter started having nightmares. I felt awful about it! It brought back all of my childhood memories of lying awake in my own bed at night and being so afraid I didn't even want to breathe heavily. Because I knew how tormenting that was, I would let her come and sleep in my room until she fell asleep, and then her father would carry her back to her own bedroom.

This started happening every night, and sometimes two and three times a night. I was really at a loss and had no idea what to do. I was exhausted, and so was she. I cried out to God for help, and after a period of time, He gave a Word of Knowledge through Dana. The word from the Lord highlighted the fact that I had yet to deal with my own fear, and that fear was opening the door for the enemy to attack my child! Yet, once I dealt with my own fear, I would be able to help my child become free from fear also.

Wow! Looking back, it seems so obvious, but it was really not clear to me at all during that time. The fear had completely paralyzed and confused me so much that I couldn't even see the truth of the situation going on in my own home. God is so good! He meets us wherever we are at, even in our confusion and fear. We just have to open our hearts and receive. So, I began to pray and seek God about how to release the fear that satan had sown into my heart as a child. The Holy Spirit spoke to me and led me to the root, which was mistrust. I had not been trusting God and had been trying to control everything in my own strength. I had to ask God for forgiveness, and from then on choose to trust Him. I then commanded the Spirit of fear to leave in the name of Jesus, and it left me!

I am still walking out this freedom. Even today, if I feel fear returning- because satan will always try to see what he can get away with- I speak the truth of God's Word to my heart and choose to trust Him. He is a good Father! I also prayed for my daughter and commanded her fear to go in the name of Jesus. I didn't need to find her root cause, as my own fear was the root cause. The nightmares immediately stopped. She has not had a nightmare since! She and I are completely set free thanks to the prompting of the Holy Spirit. Praise God!

Chapter 3
Consent and Cooperation

There are other ways to give the enemy consent and cooperation to come into your home in addition to fear. I will discuss them in this chapter.

Sin is the first and most obvious way. If you choose the enemy's stuff such as offense, anger, strife, sexual sin, or watching ungodliness on the television, your laptop, or your phone, you open up a legal door to the enemy. You have consented and cooperated through your choice to watch the ungodliness or act in an ungodly way. But don't lose heart. We have all missed it. If you have watched something, or have done something sinful, just repent quickly. Your repentance closes the door on the enemy and his legal right to come into your life and home. This is one of the reasons that the Lord says in 1 Peter 1:16, "Be holy for I am holy". He is protecting us from opening up doors to the enemy.

Imagine that we are walking around with a bubble around ourselves, protecting us from any attack of the enemy. Now, if we decide to sin, or agree with any unholy thought the enemy tries to plant in our minds, then we open up the bubble through our choice, and the enemy has the legal right to come in and attack.

In the same way, we are the gatekeepers of our home. If you think that you can watch ungodliness on your TV in the privacy of your bedroom and it doesn't affect your children, you are wrong. Electronics such as televisions, phones, and laptops are all portals. A portal is defined as a door or a gate that allows entry. These particular portals can allow entrance to the spirit realm to enter into your life, whether for good or evil. Whatever you watch, you give that permission to enter into your home. Have you noticed that the atmosphere of your home changes depending on what you have playing on your TV? What you choose to watch can bring fear, lust, or anxiety into your home. Conversely, if you have worship music playing, or an anointed minister teaching, it can also bring in the very presence and anointing of the Lord.

You may think that it is fine to watch ungodliness on your TV once the kids go to bed, yet if you could see into the Spirit realm, you would actually see the demons you just let into the home. Now they are free to go and attack your children. Unfortunately, you have allowed it.

Be vigilant, therefore, but don't make choices based on fear. Make choices based on obedience to the Holy Spirit. He is always speaking to you. Follow His leading. Follow His peace. If you don't have peace about watching something, even though your flesh still may *want* to, then deny your flesh, and obey the Spirit. He sees the dangers that you do not, and He will always keep you safe and on the right path.

If you have been watching something you didn't have peace about watching, don't worry. Just turn it off and repent quickly. Kick the enemy back out of your home and obey the Holy Spirit in the future.

One great tip I received about deciding what I should and shouldn't watch on TV is this: If Jesus can't watch it with you, then you shouldn't be watching it.

Wisdom with TV and Electronics

I teach this to my children, especially as they get older. Two of my six children are teenagers now. We don't have regular or cable TV, and we haven't had them for about nine years. I got rid of them because I couldn't control what was shown on TV. Even when we watched a wholesome movie with the kids, the ads that would come on were so inappropriate for children. But by the time I had seen it and could act, they had already seen it too, and the damage had already been done. It made me angry.

Now we just let the kids watch YouTube streamed to the TV. There is a whole lot of amazing content on YouTube, but there is also a whole lot of junk. The main thing I appreciate about YouTube is that we can choose what we want to watch and what we don't. It's much easier to screen the content before we watch it.

I taught my teenagers about how the TV is a portal and whatever you watch on it opens up a door for either God or the enemy to enter into our home. I taught them to follow the peace of God as they were choosing what to watch. I also shared with them how, when we had regular TV, and let it play non-stop without being discerning about what we were watching, my soul would feel awful. This feeling was similar to how my body would feel if I just ate junk food all day.

I shared that story with them to illustrate that even if something is not ungodly, per se, it is still not a good idea to watch a lot of frivolous content. Just like it's true in the natural realm that 'you are what you eat,' it is also true in the spirit realm that 'what you enter into, enters into you.' That means that whatever you choose to listen to, or watch, enters into your 'ear gates' and your 'eye gates,' and then directly into your soul. Then it becomes a part of who you are, how you think, and the future choices you will make.

My firstborn daughter, named Kiera, is seventeen now. She has always been able to see into the spirit realm easily. She let me know that one time she was watching a kid's show on TV when a demonic-looking black hand started reaching out of the screen. She saw it and immediately turned off the show. The hand then quickly faded out of sight.

She says that now, as she is scrolling through YouTube trying to decide what to watch, she will look at a video thumbnail and listen to the Holy Spirit to see whether or not she has peace - or the 'green light' from the Holy Spirit - before she clicks on it. Sometimes, the Lord will say to her, "Don't watch that." As long as she listens to the Lord, she knows she is safe, and nothing from the enemy will gain entry into our home.

I also should mention that I have a premium paid subscription for YouTube so we don't have any ads show up on YouTube anymore either. These ads can be just as bad as regular TV ads.

Inanimate Objects

So, we have discussed three ways the enemy can legally gain entry into our homes:

1. through our thought-life when we partner with the thoughts the enemy tries to plant in our minds,
2. through sins that are unconfessed and unrepented,
3. or, through what we choose to watch on our TV and other home devices.

Another way the enemy can gain access to our home is through inanimate objects that we have brought into our home.

One night I was on the phone with my sister-in-law. While we were chatting, we both heard my oldest daughter, Kiera, let out a blood-curdling scream from her bed where she had been sleeping. Kiera was about two or three years old at the time. I ran into the room to comfort her. She was too young to tell me what had happened. My sister-in-law said that I needed to do a thorough screening of all Kiera's toys. I had never even thought of doing that before. She said to go through them all and listen to the Holy Spirit about each one and decide which ones I have peace about and which ones I don't. She then said to throw away the ones that I didn't have peace about. One of the toys that I threw out that night was a stuffed Scooby-Doo toy. I never made the connection before, but Scooby Doo's focus is always on ghosts, monsters, and being afraid.

I've also learned that it is necessary to cleanse things in the spirit that you get from the store and especially second-hand stores. This includes clothes, books, toys, trinkets, etc. They can carry residue from the enemy on them from what the previous owner had allowed in their home or spoken around the objects because words are powerful. Just hold your hand over the object and declare, "I take authority over all darkness, and I cleanse this item for the use of the Kingdom of Heaven in the name of Jesus."

Likewise, I should have cleansed our first home when we moved into it since you never know what happens in a house while other people live there. When we arrived to live there, we didn't command the enemy to leave, nor did we cleanse the home in the name of Jesus. So, the enemy just stayed.

It is not only important to cleanse items and homes, but also hotel rooms and public seating, etc. Last year, we moved back onto a military base for about seven months. The Housing Office happily let us know that they had just completely renovated our home. I knew what that meant! I told Will that the first thing that we would do when we got there would be to cleanse it for the Kingdom. And that is what we did. And we didn't have any manifestations of the enemy in that home. Our neighbor there ended up confirming to us just how unruly the previous tenants of our home were. It was a testament to the power of the Lord to cleanse it upon our arrival.

Months later, I was on a social media page that connected all the residents of that particular military base. One of the other tenants asked everyone if anyone had any sage that she could borrow. She had 'ghosts,' as she called them, messing in her home and opening and closing doors. She wanted the sage to rid her house of them because the Base Chaplain wouldn't come to her house for a couple of days to 'bless her home.'

I thought to myself how sad it was that she was so in the dark about the spirit realm. Sage doesn't get rid of anything. It's just a plant! And if the Chaplain even knows the Lord and uses his authority to evict the demons, not 'ghosts,' from their home, the demons would just return directly afterward because they have a legal right to be there.

Not only can inanimate objects carry ungodly spiritual residue from previous owners, but some objects are just 'of the enemy,' so to speak. Certain objects in the marketplace are objects that the enemy puts into the marketplace for the sole purpose of gaining entry into your home so he can steal, kill, and destroy.

Don't try to 'cleanse' these items. Throw them away *outside* of your home, immediately. Once it is outside of your home, the enemy attached to it, loses its right to be in your home.

Also, do not give these items to someone else. In Acts 19:19, it reads, "Also, many of those who had practiced magic brought their books together and burned *them* in the sight of all. And they counted up the value of them, and *it* totaled fifty thousand *pieces* of silver." The Jews and Greeks that lived in Ephesus knew that their books about magic were evil, and it wasn't wise for the books to stay intact and therefore create a risk of falling into the hands of someone else. Once they were burned, the enemy could no longer use them..

It is impossible to list all the objects that could possibly be demonic, but that's where the Holy Spirit is so important. Ask the Holy Spirit about each object that you are about to buy or that someone is giving to you before you bring it into your home. Some of the obvious demonic items that come to mind are New Age books, books about magic, books from other religions, skulls, monster dolls, ghost dolls, items with demonic symbols on them, clothing or bedding with demonic symbols on them, artifacts from other religions, Halloween decorations, horror movies, Buddha statues, Harry Potter books or merchandise, etc.

What Kiera Saw that Night

Recently, I brought 'the screaming incident' back up to Kiera. She is now old enough to tell me what had happened that night. She said that she had woken up because something felt funny. She looked and saw 'bugs' running under her bed - this was in the spirit; they weren't natural bugs. She then went to lay her head back down and saw a black snake poke his head up from under her pillow and hiss loudly at her - this was also in the spirit. That is when she screamed.

It's easy for us parents not to take our children seriously when they tell us that they've seen something. Just because we don't see it doesn't mean that they don't. The spirit realm is very real. It is more real than what you can see, hear, taste, smell, and feel with your natural senses. Jesus said in Matthew 15:14, "Let them alone. They are blind leaders of the blind. And if the blind leads the blind, both will fall into a ditch." We don't want to be blind in our walk with the Lord, or in leading our children. We want to be able to see clearly so that we can lead our children safely around all the pitfalls of the enemy.

The Bible also says in 1 Peter 5:8, "Be sober, be vigilant; because your adversary the devil walks about like a roaring lion, seeking whom he may devour." Therefore, it is not good for us to try to raise our kids without considering the spirit realm. It affects our daily lives, whether or not we want to admit it.

The Sighing in My Home

The Holy Spirit just reminded me of something that happened recently in my home. Kiera and Jerome, my two eldest children, let me know that they heard a loud sigh every time they went upstairs into my bedroom when no one was there. I couldn't make sense of it. I don't allow the enemy in my room. My husband and I are careful about what we allow in our home. I didn't know what it could be.

During that same time, I had been dealing with depression. It wasn't a strong and debilitating depression, but it was still depression. But I noticed that I would be fine when I was downstairs with my kids, but as soon as I would head upstairs into my bedroom to get dressed and ready for the day, I lost all motivation. I would just get to my room and then sit on my bed and feel depressed. Because of this, it took me a long time to get ready and do the things I needed to do. I am usually a very tidy person, but I had not tidied up my room in a while, nor made my bed every day like I used to.

One morning the penny dropped, so to speak. I walked up to my room to get ready, as usual, and when I got upstairs, I sat on my bed and let out a loud, depressed sigh. Then the Lord reminded me about what my kids had said and the 'sighing' they had heard in my room. I had my 'lightbulb' moment. I was dealing with a spirit of depression!

Once I knew what I was dealing with, it was easy to take care of it. The Bible says in James 4:7, "Therefore submit to God. Resist the devil and he will flee from you." I just simply came out of agreement with him and resisted him. I said, "Spirit of depression, I command you to go in Jesus' name!" At once, I was sitting in the same place, but I had a totally different outlook on life. The thoughts of depression left me immediately, and I was in peace, hope, and joy once again. I also had the motivation to clean my room and make my bed once again.

The Enemy Wasn't Done

Then, a few days later, I had just woken up in the morning from a restful sleep. The first thoughts I had were thoughts of depression again. But this time, I was vigilant. I recognized them for what they were; They were not my thoughts but thoughts the enemy was giving to me. If I received the thoughts and agreed with them, I would give the enemy my consent and cooperation to come and afflict me again with depression. Instead, I quickly said, "No! Spirit of depression, I command you to go in Jesus' name!" It quickly left.

Thank God for the Holy Spirit, Who is with us always. He will make you aware of the enemy's plans so that you can also resist him and stay free.

Be vigilant against thoughts that do not line up with God's Word. Thoughts of fear, lack, lust, dissatisfaction with what God has blessed you with, and the list goes on and on.

So, as you can see, if I wasn't aware of the spirit realm, I wouldn't have been able to get victory in this area as quickly as I did... or at all, for that matter. When you don't know what you're fighting against, you can't win.

The Lord will also show us when the enemy is trying to afflict our children. Whenever one of my children is dealing with something, I sit down with them and hear their hearts. Once I have listened to what is on their heart, I pray in tongues and wait to hear what the Lord will show me. I try not to assume anything. The Lord reveals to me what is going on in the spirit realm or in my child's heart, and once He does, I can properly minister to my kids and can pray directly to the heart of the issue. In this way, I can nip every issue in the bud.

One time, for example, one of my daughters was upset at one of her siblings. I heard her heart and prayed for wisdom. The Lord showed me that she had unforgiveness in her heart towards that sibling and that unforgiveness had manifested a spirit of anger in my daughter. We were able to pray together to release the offense and command the spirit of anger to leave. I was then able to minister to her about how to stay out of offense in the future. It is powerful when you work *with* the Holy Spirit.

A man of God gave my husband and me a prophecy while we were at Bible College. He said, "You and Will will spring every trap of the enemy that he has set for your children." It was a powerful and comforting prophecy. And I can see that through what the Lord has revealed to me about His Word and the spirit realm, coupled with seeking His counsel when situations arise, we will always foil the enemy's plans, and my children will remain free from his plots.

Watch Out for Strife

I want to be very open and honest about my life and struggles to help you to be aware of other ways that the enemy can gain entrance into your home. In the past, I had struggled a lot with taking offense with the things that my husband said, did, or didn't do. And I have noticed that when I got offended at my husband for something, it opened a door to the enemy.

Just for the record, I have an amazing husband. These things that I got offended over were super small things, mainly misunderstandings. Also, I am normally a peaceful person - there are just always opportunities to get into offense. Jesus said in Luke 17:1 that it is impossible that no offenses should come. They are a fact of life. But we still have a choice about how we respond to them.

So, there are things that I have noticed that happen after I get offended at my husband when the issue hasn't been resolved.

One of the things that happen is that when I try to go to sleep, the enemy keeps me awake. I start to doze off and then I get an itch on a part of my body, such as my face. This wakes me up, and I have to scratch it. Then when I start to doze off again, I will get another itch on another part of my body, such as my leg. Then I have to scratch that itch. It just keeps happening over and over, and it keeps me awake and brings a lot of frustration. When I repent and make things right with my husband, the itching stops, and I can sleep.

Another thing that happens is that right as I start to doze off, I get shocked awake by a sound that my husband doesn't hear. It's super strange. Sometimes I can't even discern what sound it was. It's hard to describe. Maybe you know what I'm talking about. I'm about to doze off and then get shocked right out of that place and have to start falling asleep right from the beginning.

Another thing that happens is that I start seeing images of things appearing before my eyes in my imagination. As I described earlier, when you see something in your imagination, it is actually right there in front of you in the spirit realm, and you're seeing it with your spiritual vision.

So, when I start seeing demonic images, I know that those things are literally in my house. For instance, one night, I started seeing one demonic-looking clown after another. One night I saw a translucent spider descending in front of me as if it were descending from a web. Sometimes I see ugly faces or skulls and black things. They're obviously not holy things sent from the Lord.

When I start seeing these things, I realize that I have opened a door to these things. I repent of strife and offense and then command the enemy to go. He always goes. The Scripture says in James 3:16 KJV, "For where envying and strife is, there is confusion and *every evil work.*" (Emphasis mine.) So, when I open the door to strife, I open the door to confusion and every evil work. The New King James Version of the Bible uses the word 'self-seeking' instead of the word 'strife.' That's powerful. When we consider others above ourselves, we don't open the door to strife.

Another thing happens when I unwittingly open the door to offense and strife. It unfortunately also affects my kids. One particular night I was offended at my husband about something, and then my teenage daughter, Kiera, texted me from her bedroom. My daughter is a Seer - she has always been able to see and hear things easily in the spirit realm. She asked me what was going on in the house because she saw demonic things in her room, and an item in her room was also just knocked over. This was eye-opening to me. Along with my husband, I am a gatekeeper of my home. I decide what is allowed in and what has to stay out. I usher in the presence of the Lord, and I keep the enemy out. Unfortunately, I had failed. I had allowed the enemy into my home, and he now had access to my kids, too. I quickly repented and commanded the enemy to leave, and my daughter told me in the morning that the rest of the night was peaceful for her.

I had to get a handle on my emotions and not allow strife into my home. So I decided to ask the Lord when it was that a disagreement turns into strife and opens the door to the enemy.

He responded, "You open the door when you respond in the flesh and don't leave room for the Spirit. You act hastily and without forethought of the consequences to the atmosphere of your home. The enemy gains access and enters the conversation. To combat this, never act on impulse. Respond in the Spirit because that's where Truth and Liberty exist. It will close the door to the enemy completely. Therefore, raising your voice in anger is never a good thing. It always works against you. Yield to My Spirit and obey My voice in your situation."

What the Bible Says

The Bible has this to say about anger and strife:

> James 1:20 NASB "For a man's anger does not bring about the righteousness of God."
>
> James 1:19 NASB "You know *this*, my beloved brothers *and sisters*. Now everyone must be quick to hear, slow to speak, *and* slow to anger."
>
> Proverbs 10:19 "In the multitude of words sin is not lacking, But he who restrains his lips *is* wise."
>
> Ephesians 4:26,27 "'Be angry, and do not sin': do not let the sun go down on your wrath, nor give place to the devil."
>
> Galatians 5:16 "I say then: Walk in the Spirit, and you shall not fulfill the lust of the flesh."

These are powerful Scriptures. The Lord has shown me that when the feeling of anger arises in me, or I get hurt and begin to feel offense, to ask the Lord, "Lord, what do You say about this situation?" And then act on what He says. Also, pray in the Spirit and be cautious of your thoughts. The enemy can give you thoughts that compound the thoughts that you are already having and increase your anger. Have you noticed that too? You could be angry at one thing, and then you start thinking about everything else that your husband has done wrong in the past. Then you can't think of anything that he has done right. This is the enemy.

To combat this, you need to first be aware of what is really happening in the spirit and then control your thoughts. When you control your thoughts, then you can control your emotions and your actions. Your emotions and actions *always* follow your thoughts. Therefore, if you change what you *think* about the situation, you will change your *actions*. And remember, your spouse is not your enemy. The devil is. He hates marriage and tries everything to cause a rift in your union and then exploits it to try to tear your marriage and family apart. And yes, it's *that* serious. Marriage is a picture of Christ and His church. The enemy hates it.

So, as warfare, start thinking about the things that you are thankful for in your husband. Recall positive memories to mind. Say about the offense, "That is such a small thing." All these things help to quickly change your emotions. Don't let the enemy control what you're thinking about and drive you into a rage.

My Victory

Even though I knew about the dangers of offense and what I *should* do when an opportunity for offense rears its ugly head, I still couldn't seem to do the right thing. I want to share with you what finally helped me to get freedom and victory in this area in the hope that it might be what helps you too.

It all started when I was listening to the minister, Kevin Zadai. Kevin died on the operating table and spent 45 minutes in Heaven receiving revelation from Jesus, Himself. I have received so much powerful revelation from Kevin's ministry.

Kevin tells a story about how he was challenged by someone who said to him, "You act like there is a demon behind every tree." Kevin responded to him, "There is *not* a demon behind every tree – there are seven!" He also shares that when he talks to astronauts, the astronauts share that when they get high up in the earth's atmosphere, they can really hear God clearer, like there is no hindrance of the enemy there. That showed me that we have more hindrances from the enemy here than we realize.

He also shares that while he was in Heaven, he really saw how much the enemy interfered in our everyday lives and how hard it was to live down here. So, when the Lord Jesus told Kevin to go back to earth, Kevin told Him that he did not want to go. When Kevin changed his mind and decided that he would go back, he made a plan of how he was going to stay ahead of the enemy and not allow the enemy to attack him and interfere in his life. He said that he was going to do certain things such as: live a holy life and pray in tongues as much as possible.

Kevin also goes on to explain that the spirit realm is very fast. As soon as you pray, God answers. However, it is the enemy that hinders the prayers. He stands in the way and tries to keep the answer from you until you *hopefully* lose faith and give up believing.

All of this opened my eyes to what the enemy was really doing behind the scenes of my life. I started to pay attention to my thoughts and analyze them to make sure that the enemy wasn't making me believe things that weren't true. I then quickly realized that he had been playing me like a fiddle! I was acutely aware that every time an offense was presented to me, I took the bait! I can just imagine the enemy laughing at me. I also realized that, because I had given it to him, the enemy had the power to get me into offense any time that he wanted to.

This made me mad! I couldn't believe that I had been such a fool and given the enemy so much power over me! I decided then and there that I wasn't going to allow the enemy to get me into offense like that again. And praise God! This was finally the revelation that gave me my victory!! Right now, I hear the Lord quoting John 8:32, "And you shall know the truth, and the truth shall make you free." And Hosea 4:6, "My people are destroyed for lack of knowledge."

When we have our eyes opened to the truth, we can no longer be deceived.

I now fully realized that my husband was *never* the enemy, and I also realized how much power I had been giving to the *real* enemy this whole time.

How the Enemy Works

This is how the enemy works: He will set out a trap of offense and wait for you to take the bait. Your husband may do something in the innocence of his heart, but then the enemy comes along and gives you negative thoughts about your husband and his motives. He will accuse and slander your husband and even remind you of things from the past that compound the offense! If you agree with the enemy's accusations, he gains power. He will continue to lie and accuse and slander so long as you keep agreeing with him. Now, in your anger, you go and speak to your husband. Your husband doesn't appreciate the disrespect, and he tries to defend himself. Yet, you can't understand his point of view because of your anger and your negative mindset. Now, the enemy has the two of you pitted against each other while he just sits back and laughs. Does this sound familiar?

Yet, since I have had this revelation, I have been able to let offenses slide off like water off a duck's back. And if there is actually an issue that needs to be addressed, not just a misunderstanding, I can just go to my husband and start a conversation about it and not an argument. I even say to my husband, "I know you are not the enemy here, and I just wanted to let you know that even though it probably wasn't your intention, I felt hurt when you said/did this." And he then can share his heart on what he meant or even apologize for his words/actions coming across that way.

Another great tip is to pray over the conversation before you have it. You can pray like this: "Heavenly Father, I thank You that you are with me, and You guide me into all truth and out of every trap set for me by the enemy. Lord, You see that I am about to have a conversation with my husband. Please give me the right words to say and help my husband see my heart. Help my words to be seasoned with grace and make sure that there are no misunderstandings between us. And right now, I take power and authority over all the power of the enemy, and I cancel the enemy's assignments against myself, my husband, our marriage, and our family. Enemy, I forbid you to speak to my husband or myself during this conversation. You cannot warp our words or cause any division between us in Jesus' name!" You will find that your conversations are much more fruitful when the enemy is not meddling.

I am only sharing about offense because we, as parents, need to watch over our children and keep them safe from the wiles of the enemy. And this is one of the ways he tries to gain entrance. He tries to get parents at odds with one another to open the door to come into the home. When parents are in unity with each other and walking in peace and joy while staying vigilant against the enemy, the enemy cannot come in at all. We want our kids to grow up in a home filled with peace and joy and the atmosphere of Heaven. We don't want them to have unnecessary struggles because their parents always respond in the flesh instead of walking in the spirit.

I don't want you to feel condemned about this. As you can see, I have missed it many times. However, when I realize what I've done, I *quickly* repent and ask the Lord for forgiveness, and I command the enemy to leave.

Below is a sample prayer of what I personally pray if I do take the bait of offense. I sometimes even pray this quietly under my breath, but it is still just as powerful. I heard someone once say, "Keep short accounts." So, I encourage you to endeavor to live a holy life on purpose, but if you sin, then repent quickly. Don't allow any time to pass where you have not repented and thus have allowed the enemy to come in and mess with you and your family.

My prayer is as follows:

> "Heavenly Father, I repent for taking offense and getting into strife with my husband. I am sorry. I ask for Your forgiveness, and I receive Your forgiveness in Jesus' name. As an act of my will, I choose to loose all strife and offense from my soul right now in Jesus' name."

And just as another quick tip, I talk about loosing things from your soul in the next chapter. So this will make more sense as you read on, but when you start feeling a feeling of anger or being upset with your spouse, you can choose to loose that offense/anger from your soul before you even *feel* like it. One time I was sitting in bed, and my husband said something that upset me. I could start to feel those familiar feelings rise up within me. I knew I had taken offense, and I couldn't shake it. I then remembered that I could loose it from my soul without feeling like it first, and only as an act of obedience to the Father. I decided to honor God above my feelings, and I said under my breath, "Heavenly Father, I repent of taking offense, and as an act of my will, I choose to loose all offense from my soul, in Jesus' name you go!" Immediately my feelings changed! I was so surprised. I no longer had offense and was able to keep the door shut to the enemy.

If you are skeptical and you think that the enemy is not entering into your conversations. I will give you a Scripture to help you understand. The Lord just gave this to me as I was praying and asking the Lord for an example that I can give to you.

Do you remember Matthew 16:23, where Jesus turned to Peter and said, "Get behind Me, satan"? It was Peter talking, so why did Jesus address satan? Because Jesus knew that the words that Peter just spoke were not from Peter at all. What the enemy does is he speaks to us and gives us thoughts and words to speak. We don't know that those words are inspired by the devil, and in the heat of an argument, you speak them out. Have you ever said something in the heat of an argument that you didn't mean and later regretted it? That's why we have to be so careful not to get into the flesh and operate through our emotions. Jesus wants us to keep a tight grip on the words that we speak because life and death are in the power of our tongue. (Proverbs 18:21) We want to stay vigilant to not become a mouthpiece for the enemy. Not every thought that comes into your mind originated from you. Sometimes it is the Lord speaking to us, and other times it is the enemy. So, we need to use wisdom and think before we speak.

Chapter 4
Powerful Spiritual Truths

In this chapter, I will make you aware of other tactics of the enemy aimed towards ourselves and our children.

Firstly, we have power over *all* the power of the enemy, and nothing shall by any means hurt us, according to Luke 10:19.

We never need to be afraid of the enemy for any reason. Jesus completely defeated him on the cross. His power against us has been stripped from him. Now his only weapon is deceit. As long as we *believe* he can do something to us, that is the only way he can. But as you can see, he is using *our* power to accomplish it because we have *faith* that he can.

Unbelief in what God has said to us is just simply faith in what the enemy is saying instead. It's just faith in the wrong direction.

What we Look Like in the Spirit

I will let you know a little story that illustrates this. As I am writing this portion of the book, we live in a two-story home with a finished basement. My bedroom is on the top floor, and my oldest daughter, Kiera, is staying in the basement. One day, my husband was away for work and wasn't home for the night. Kiera came upstairs to tell me that there were demons in her room with red eyes, and they were sitting on her bed. She wanted me to come and deal with them.

As I said, my husband wasn't home and so I knew that I had to be brave and go down there to deal with them myself. My husband has seen a lot of demonic manifestations in his life, and it doesn't rattle him. He just knows who he is in Christ and takes care of business. For myself, however, it has been a journey.

I started to head down the two flights of stairs to walk into a room infested with demons. As I was walking down the stairs, I was feeling very small, and I saw the enemy, in my imagination, as very big and intimidating. Then the Lord brought something to my remembrance. Years ago, I had asked Him what I look like in the Spirit. He showed me a vision. In the vision, I was standing in an open field. I was gigantic - probably the height of a two-story building. I was standing with a resolute look on my face, with all my armor on and ready for battle. The enemy was about the size of a cockroach compared to me. All I did was calmly walk forward, and I easily crushed the enemy under my feet. It was effortless!

So, the Lord brought this to my remembrance. I immediately went from feeling like a weak and powerless little girl that was afraid about what she was about to walk into to a formidable warrior knowing that the enemy was actually terrified of *her*!

I thought to myself, "Right!" and I walked into Kiera's room with boldness! I took authority over the enemy and commanded them all to leave. And that was that! Kiera, who can see into the Spirit Realm, told me afterward that the demons in her room were very large and intimidating looking. But as soon as I took my authority, they shrunk to the size of cockroaches and scattered quickly out of the house (the same way that natural cockroaches scatter when you turn on the light).

I was ministering to Kiera later about the truth that 'whatever you focus on expands.' When you focus on the Lord, He expands in your life, and you get more of Him. But the same is also true for the enemy. As she focused on them and gave them her attention, and allowed fear to enter in, they appeared a lot larger than they actually were.

I hope that encouraged you. It doesn't matter *what* the enemy is doing in your house or how he is manifesting, at the name of Jesus, he will *flee* from you! He won't be able to escape fast enough! Know who you are and know your authority!

The Bible confirms this in James 4:7 KJV, "Submit yourselves therefore to God, resist the enemy and he will flee from you."

Your Soul

Another important truth is that God gave you a 'will', and it resides in your soul. Your soul contains your mind, your will, and your emotions. God didn't create robots. He could have created robots, but He wanted children that would *choose* to love Him, not children who are *forced* to love Him. So, we can use our will to choose God and the things of God, or we can use it to reject God and thus choose the enemy and the things of the enemy. Also, your 'heart', which the Scripture talks about, is both your spirit and your soul together; It is the 'heart' of your being.

Most of the time, we get to choose what we see, hear, and experience - and whatever we see, hear, or experience goes into our soul and becomes a part of us. This is a good thing when it is things originating from God, such as love, joy, peace, happy experiences, kind words, and empowering messages. It's not so good when people have done or said things that have hurt us and have caused trauma. It is also not good if we have watched or said things ourselves that were ungodly or negative. It all goes into our souls and becomes a part of who we are. Remember the phrase, "What you enter into, enters into you"? Whatever you choose, whether good or bad, goes into your soul. Your soul is your mind, will, and emotions, right? So, whatever is in your soul will be what you think about, what you decide to choose again, and what will affect your emotions.

When we choose things of the enemy, we allow those things to enter into our souls. Our choices are what 'open the door' to him. We have allowed him in. He now has the legal right to negatively affect us.

Jesus never chose any of the enemy's stuff, and that is why He could say in John 14:30 "I will no longer talk much with you, for the ruler of this world is coming, and *he has nothing in Me.*" (Emphasis, mine). We need to also make sure that when the enemy comes to us, there is nothing of him in us either!

Sometimes it is not our fault. Sometimes a wrong has been done to us, and it wasn't something that we have chosen for ourselves. But unfortunately, it is still in our soul and negatively affects us.

Hang in there. This has a good ending.

We Have the Keys of the Kingdom

Jesus said in Matthew 16:19, "And I will give you the keys of the kingdom of heaven, and whatever you bind on earth will be bound in heaven, and whatever you loose on earth will be loosed in heaven."

This Scripture shows us that *whatever* we bind on earth will be bound in heaven, and *whatever* we loose on earth will be loosed in heaven. The things that we have allowed in our soul certainly qualify as a "whatever."

Through an act of our will, which is the power that God gave us to *choose*, we can decide to loose the bad things *from* our soul and bind the good things *to* our soul. The words, 'bind' and 'loose' were common in Jewish legal language. Bind means 'to declare something to be allowed,' whereas loose means 'to declare something to be forbidden.'

Paul spoke in 1 Corinthians 7:27 and said, "Are you bound to a wife? Do not seek to be loosed. Are you loosed from a wife? Do not seek a wife." In this, we see that when we bind, we bind things *to* ourselves, and when we loose, we loose things *from* ourselves.

Therefore, when we bind things to our soul, we are declaring it to be allowed in our soul, and heaven comes into agreement with us. Similarly, when we loose something from our soul, we are declaring it to be forbidden from our soul, and heaven comes into agreement with us.

When we use these keys of the Kingdom to bind to, and loose from, our souls, then we will have what 3 John 2 says, "Beloved, I pray that you may prosper in all things and be in health, just as your soul prospers." So, if we flip that backward, we see that *even as our soul prospers, we will prosper.* We cannot prosper unless our soul is prospering.

The Scripture also says in Proverbs 4:23, "Keep your heart with all diligence, for out of it *spring* the issues of life." Your heart is the core of your 'Spirit Man' - the spiritual part of you. We need to choose carefully what we allow into our heart/soul because all of the issues of life come from our heart from what we have allowed in there.

So many of us are not prospering because of what we have in our souls. Because of the negative things which are in our soul, it affects what we think about, what we choose, and the emotions we display. It can even affect our health. Have you ever wondered why a woman, who just gets out of an abusive relationship, ends up choosing the same type of man again? Or why you, or your children, keep having recurring nightmares about some trauma in the past, and you can't stop? Or why people are stuck in the cycle of addiction no matter how hard they try to get free? It's because it is in your soul.

Once you get it out of your soul, you will be free, and now you will prosper and be in health.

I know a man who struggled with drinking alcohol on a daily basis. He wanted to stop but wasn't able to. I led him through a prayer in which he repented of choosing alcohol as a coping mechanism instead of running to the Lord for help.

In the prayer, he also loosed alcohol addiction and all desire for alcohol from his soul. Immediately, he lost the taste for alcohol. He tried to drink, but it didn't even taste good to him anymore. Within just a few days, he was completely free of needing alcohol. Praise the Lord!

Here is another powerful example of how loosing things from your soul can really make all the difference. About a year ago, there was this demon-looking animation that someone uploaded on YouTube, called 'Momo.' This hideous character would show up on the YouTube advertisements and ask the children to play a game. It would say that they couldn't tell their parents about the game, or 'she' would come into their house and kill their parents. If the kids played the game, out of fear of her threats, she would ask the kids to do certain dangerous things around the house such as leave the stove on at night, and things like that. Momo was incredibly hideous and frightening to even look at - even for me.

My daughter, Kiera, had seen the ad pop up. She told me about it - to her credit - but she was in a lot of fear about it. When she would go to bed at night, she would see, with her spiritual sight, Momo in her bedroom! I told her to command it to go, but she kept seeing it night after night. I wasn't sure why. Kiera then had the idea to loose all the images and fear of Momo from her soul. She did that, and she never 'saw' Momo again.

Maybe your child is dealing with fear or torment on a nightly basis, or with insecurities or believing certain lies about themselves, and you've prayed for them, but nothing seems to be helping. The Holy Spirit is key to help you to know what the root cause of this is.

Here is a testimony of something else that Kiera went through and how we came out the other side victoriously.

Freedom from Abandonment

When my firstborn, Kiera, was five years old, her younger brother, Jerome, was four years old, and I was pregnant with Grace. My husband was in the US Army, and we had just received the news that he would be sent on a deployment to Haiti. He was sent on a humanitarian mission to help the citizens of Haiti after the devastating earthquake in 2010.

Instead of leaving the kids and me on the military base in Louisiana all alone with no family around, he sent us back to Australia so that I could be with my family and I could give birth in Australia while he was gone. I moved in with my younger sister, Stephanie, and her husband, Paul, who were expecting their first baby.

Stephanie ended up giving birth to her son, Ezekiel, only ten days before I gave birth to Grace. My older sister, Kerry, was going to drive from her house to come and pick me up and then drive me to the hospital when it was time for me to give birth. Stephanie was going to watch Kiera and Jerome for me while I was gone until my parents could come and get them.

We had a plan!

Early one morning when it was still dark, I started getting contractions, and I knew that my time had come. I called Kerry, and she got in her car and started the drive to come and get me. Kiera and Jerome were still asleep, and I had a thought to wake them up to let them know that I was leaving, but I was having a lot of contractions, and the labor was getting intense already. (I gave birth in two and a half hours altogether!)

So, I let Stephanie know that I was leaving, and I headed to the hospital. Stephanie had planned to get up at 7 am to be up for Kiera and Jerome, but because she was tired after taking care of her newborn all night, she slept in. Kiera and Jerome woke up in the morning and then walked into my room but couldn't find me. So, they walked around the house and couldn't find me there either. They both started screaming at the top of their lungs and started banging their fists against Stephanie and Paul's bedroom door. Stephanie said that she let the kids into her room, and she held one of my children, and Paul held the other one while they both tried to calm them down and reassure them. They told me that it took them a long time to calm them down. After that time, Kiera and Jerome were in a lot of fear, even after I came home from the hospital with their new baby sister. I could not even put them in the back of the car and shut the door just to quickly go to the driver's seat of the car without them screaming loudly in fear.

When I would leave my parent's house, my parents would have to come outside with me. Once I put Kiera and Jerome in the car, they would have to stand next to each child to comfort them so that I could get in the driver's seat to go home. It was wild! And on top of that, I had a newborn, and my husband was all the way in Haiti! This fear continued for months and even continued once we were reunited with Will and returned to the United States. Through prayer, the fear started to go away, and life returned to normal.

While we were still in the thick of it, I was talking to my mother about why the kids reacted as they did. She said that, from their perspective, their dad was gone, and then they woke up, and mom was gone too! It was scary for them.

The conclusion of this story happened eleven years later when Kiera was sixteen years old. As I have already said, she is a seer, meaning that she can see into the spirit realm. I have always had to pray for her at night time because of the things that she would see. When I would pray, the things would leave. I taught her how to use her own authority to command the things of the enemy to leave. She would always say that they don't listen to her and they don't leave when she tells them to. I would wonder, "How can they *not* leave? They *have to* leave." It was a regular battle.

A Revelation

When she was sixteen, Kiera came to me at night. The Lord had given her a revelation, and she came to share it with me. We were getting ready to move houses again - when I started writing this book we lived in Colorado, and since then we moved to Corpus Christi, Texas, for a few months, and now have settled into another city near San Antonio, Texas, by the leading of the Lord.

Kiera was trying to downsize her belongings and was having a hard time letting go of things that she knew she wouldn't ever need or use. She asked the Lord, "Why is it so hard for me to let go of things?" Then she started vaguely remembering that there was something in the past that she thought that she had lost. As she started to meditate on this, the Lord reminded her of the time in Australia when her dad was in Haiti and then I had left also.

In her memory, the Lord brought her all the way back to before her dad left when she saw her four-year-old brother holding onto his dad's back jean pocket and saying, "Daddy, don't go."

She remembered hearing me say, "Daddy is going to Haiti. He is going away for a long time." Then she remembered hearing, "Your dad is dead." The enemy spoke this to her. She was really confused because she said that she didn't even know what Haiti meant, and she started believing that he had died and was never coming back. Then, when she woke up that morning, and I was gone too, she thought I had died also. She had a large heart-wound, and even though none of her fears were founded, she carried that heart-wound until she was sixteen years old, and the Lord revealed this to her.

She came to me right after the Lord showed her this revelation and I discerned, through the Holy Spirit, that she had a spirit of abandonment. I immediately began to pray for her. I prayed that the Lord would heal her heart. I then loosed all the trauma of abandonment and fear from her soul and then bound to her soul the love, comfort, joy, and peace of God.

From that point on, Kiera noticed a big difference in her life, especially at night. She no longer was tormented by fear, and if the enemy tried to come to her, she would command them to go, and they would leave immediately. She was free!

Remember how Jesus said, "The ruler of this world is coming, and he has nothing in Me."? When we are wounded, the enemy has a 'landing strip,' so to speak. He has a legal right to be in your life. But when we allow the Holy Spirit to show us where we are wounded, and we forgive any perpetrators and repent of any sins, then those things are loosed from our souls. Then we can say, "There is none of him (the enemy) in me." The enemy no longer has any legal right to be in our lives, and we are free.

The Bible also says in Proverbs 26:2, "Like a flitting sparrow, like a flying swallow, So a curse without cause shall not alight." If there is no landing strip for the enemy, he cannot land on you. The curse will not alight—alight means to descend from the air and settle. So, when we are healed of all wounds, and have repented of all sins, and loosed them all from our souls, the enemy will try to descend and settle on us, but he won't be able to. Praise God!

I just heard a testimony from a fellow Bible College alumnus named Greg. Greg was praying for people at one of Andrew Wommack's events. A man came forward to be prayed for because of pain in his back. Greg prayed for this man to be free from this back pain, but the pain didn't leave. As the man left the prayer line, Greg saw the word "DAD" form in his mind on the man's back. The man returned later on that day to receive prayer once again. Greg asked the man if he had any unforgiveness towards his dad. The man replied that he didn't. He then asked if he had any issues with his dad, to which the man also responded that he did not. Greg then revealed to the man that he saw the word "DAD" form on his back as he was walking away from the prayer line earlier that same day. The man revealed to Greg that he used to be a dad before his son died. Greg then prayed for the Lord to heal the man's heart of that trauma. Once he did this, the pain in the man's back was completely healed!

The Holy Spirit will also lead and guide you into freedom in every area of your life. He wants you and your children to be free more than you do. He died so that you can be free! Trust him to lead you into all truth. Just get quiet and listen to what He shares with you. Pay attention to any images or words that alight in your imagination as you pray.

You and your husband, if you are married, are the godly authority over your children, and He will reveal to you the things concerning them. He won't leave you in the dark. He doesn't want the enemy to interfere in your lives and so He will expose the plans of the enemy without delay.

Offense

As I shared earlier in this book, when you choose offense, you are simultaneously choosing to bind it to your soul. It is important to decide not to receive any offenses in the first place. However, if you have already chosen to become offended, you can choose, even before you feel like it, to loose it from your soul. Once it is out of your soul, you won't think about it anymore, and you won't have the emotions attached to it. You will be free from the offense.

The Lord just reminded me of a testimony I heard years ago. There was a Pastor's wife who was diagnosed with cancer. After she was diagnosed with cancer, the Lord brought her attention to the fact that she was harboring a lot of offense from a whole lot of people from her past. She sat down and wrote a letter to each person repenting to them of the offense that she had taken and asked each of them for forgiveness. As she did that, she truly released all offense from her soul. Shortly afterward, she was supernaturally healed of cancer. What had occurred was that her soul had begun to prosper when she released all the offense, and now she was in health once again.

I recently heard another testimony of a lady who grew up in a home where her mother abandoned her, and her father was physically and emotionally abusive. She was also sexually abused by a member of her extended family. When she became an adult, she left home and led a promiscuous life and often broke the law. One day she went to a party and was brutally raped by two men who were then plotting how they were going to kill her. She cried out to Jesus, and He rescued her from death. She was so thankful to the Lord that she gave her life over to Jesus and decided to live for Him. A few years later, she was diagnosed with an Abdominal Aneurysm. The doctors couldn't fix it, and she was hospitalized many times because of it. One day the Lord asked her to forgive all the people who had abused and rejected her. She obeyed God and forgave everyone. Not long afterward, she felt a difference in her body. She felt like she was healed. So she went in for a CAT Scan at the hospital, and they found no trace of the Abdominal Aneurysm. She was completely healed.

I'm not saying that every sickness or disease is caused by something that needs to be loosed from one's soul, but some of them definitely *could be*.

As you can see, it is important to watch over your soul and the souls of your children. We need to take our authority and *loose from* and *bind to* their soul on their behalf. We also need to teach our older children how to do this on their own.

If our children are being bullied at school, you can loose all the fear, intimidation, and threatening or demeaning words from their souls.

Your prayer over your children would begin as follows: "As Emily's covering, I choose, as an act of my will, to loose..." The rest of the prayer is continued below.

Prayer

Here is a sample prayer to help you to get started in loosing and binding from your soul, as well as the souls of your children. Please listen to the Holy Spirit as you pray and loose or bind anything else that He speaks to you.

"Heavenly Father, I am your child. I don't want any darkness in me. So, as an act of my will, I choose to loose all darkness, all past sadnesses, all trauma and past failures, all fear, all offense, all oppression, all depression, all despair, all hate, all witchcraft, any torment, all unbelief, all hopelessness, rejection and unworthiness, all fear of man, any addictions of any kind, all vain imaginations, all memories and images of the enemy's stuff, anything that I chose that was not of You - anything of the enemy! Right now, I choose to loose it from my soul. In Jesus' name, YOU GO!

Father, I choose to send back any layers of anything or anybody else that I may have retained from experiences or relationships in my life. I sever that tie and send that back!

Father, I want my soul to be whole, so as an act of my will I call back all those parts of myself that I gave away. Right now I call them back into my soul so I can be whole. In Jesus name, COME BACK!

Father, I thank You that now that my soul is whole, I will prosper and be in health. So, right now, I bind to my soul: Your love, Your joy, Your light, Your life, Your provision, Your peace, and Your presence. In Jesus' name, I RECEIVE THEM!"

I like to pray this prayer regularly. When you walk around in this world, there is a lot of 'dust' that gets kicked up onto you. Therefore, I like to do a 'Soul Checkup' and pray this prayer again to make sure that I am free from anything of the enemy.

One day, my son Jerome came up to me. He was looking forlorn and told me that he wasn't feeling 'quite right' in his emotions. I told him to do the 'Soul Prayer.' He prayed and came back with a smile on his face and a relieved heart. He told me that he felt so much better, and he needs to remember to pray that prayer more often.

For me, I like to pray this prayer when I have let others' words affect me, and I keep pondering on them. Or if I was affected by bad news and can't get it out of my head. I also pray it when I feel fear or any other negative emotion.

One time, a family friend who was a friend of my parents since I was a little girl made a comment about me to my parents. My parents let me know what she had said. It was something negative about me homeschooling my kids. Her words were bothering me a lot throughout that day, and so I decided to loose those words from my soul. To this day, I can't recall to my mind what she actually said. Therefore, it doesn't bother me today. Those words are not a part of me, and they don't affect my decisions or my life in any way. Those words were spoken by the inspiration of the enemy to throw me off what the Lord has called me to do with my kids. But they were unfruitful!

You may have had words that were spoken over you that still run through your head and shape the decisions you make today. Loose those words from your soul and come out of agreement with them right now. Any negative words that were spoken over you were inspired by the enemy and *not* what the Lord says about you. So, loose those words from your soul and decide to believe all the wonderful things that God says about you. Remember that the enemy is the father of lies, whereas the Lord only speaks the truth.

My dad made a joke one day. He said, jokingly to my mom, "I knew it was a lie! You know how? Because your lips moved!" And this is so true for the enemy. You can guarantee that it's a lie because the enemy was the one who said it. Someone was confiding in me recently. They said that the enemy was tormenting them and saying to them that their future children were going to be born with disabilities. I replied to the person, "Well, rejoice then. Because you *know* it's a lie because it was the enemy that said it!"

The person started grinning from ear to ear. They got it! The enemy had no more power over them.

I now want to share certain spiritual situations that have come up in my family and how we navigated through them. I will also share situations that have not come up in my family but are still pretty common things to deal with.

Imaginary Friends

Even if this is something that your children haven't experienced, I am sure you have heard of other children having imaginary friends. If you are not aware of how real the spirit realm is, you would just chalk it all up to the child's imagination. Parents even cater to these 'imaginary friends' by giving them a seat at the dinner table and setting some food out for them at the request of their child. I just want you to be aware that 'imaginary friends' aren't imaginary at all. They are real beings that children can see and interact with in the spirit realm.

Children can indeed see angels and even play with them, but a lot of the time, an imaginary friend is actually a demon. Demons can also *appear* to be friendly and innocent. The Scripture says in 2 Corinthians 11:14, "And no wonder! For satan, himself transforms himself into an angel of light." If you humor your child and become a good host to the demon which is masquerading as an imaginary friend, it is dangerous for your child. Just like you would not allow your child to play with a venomous spider, you wouldn't want them to play with an imaginary friend for the same reason. Kick it out of your house ASAP! Command it to leave. Just simply say, "Imaginary friend, if you are not an angel sent by the Most High God, I take authority over you, and I command you to leave my child and my home, never to return, in the name of Jesus!"

Your child may also be influenced by a spirit that may make itself known as a 'Spirit Guide.' This is a demon that disguises itself to look innocent and guides you with its ulterior motives. Spirit Guides are *never* from God. We only have the Holy Spirit to lead and guide us. Command the "Spirit Guide" (Demon) to go in Jesus' name!

Testing Spirits

There are many other spirits in the spirit realm that can come to our children. My daughter, Kiera, has seen a whole myriad of spirits. It is important to teach your children how to test the spirits to see if they have been sent by the Lord or the enemy. The Scripture says in 1 John 4:1-3, "Beloved, do not believe every spirit, but test the spirits, whether they are of God; because many false prophets have gone out into the world. By this you know the Spirit of God: Every spirit that confesses that Jesus Christ has come in the flesh is of God, and every spirit that does not confess that Jesus Christ has come in the flesh is not of God. And this is the *spirit* of the Antichrist, which you have heard was coming, and is now already in the world."

I teach my children that when a spirit appears to them, to always ask them, "Do you confess that Jesus Christ has come in the flesh?" If the spirit says, "yes", then it is from God and can be trusted. If the spirit does not respond, then command it to go in Jesus' name. Normally, once you ask the spirit the question, if it is not from the Lord, it will simply leave. But if it just remains there and remains silent, simply command it to leave.

I have even written the following words on a piece of paper and have given it to each child to memorize, "Do you confess that Jesus Christ has come in the flesh?" It really helped them to remember what to say.

Nightmares

Sometimes you have to minister to your children who come to you in the middle of the night with nightmares. You have already read my friend's testimony of her own fear opening up the door for that same fear to attack her child with nightmares. That is one reason that nightmares could come.

The problem could also be that something they watched or experienced throughout the day is now in their soul. Dreams normally come from our souls. Whatever we meditate on and experience throughout our day can show up in our dreams at night. That's why it is important for us, as parents, to monitor what our kids are exposed to on TV. I try my best to keep my children from watching anything with monsters, ghosts, or shows with ungodly themes. Therefore, they very rarely have nightmares.

So, if your child is having nightmares because of something that they have watched, heard, or experienced, you can simply loose all of it from their souls. Once it is no longer in there, it won't appear in their dreams. I heard a story of a young girl who had constant nightmares. The nightmares were linked to a traumatic experience that she had gone through. When her mother loosed the trauma of that experience from her soul, the nightmares completely stopped.

This is what I do with my children when they come to me after a nightmare. I hug them and console them, and then I pray over them. I loose things from their soul (whatever the Holy Spirit brings to my mind) and command the spirit of fear to leave. I also bind the peace of God to their soul. It doesn't take long before they are ready to go back to bed. They wake up in the morning, and they have had no further nightmares.

Do you see why it is so important to know what is going on in the spirit realm? When you know what is really going on, you can deal with the heart of the matter and get instant results. You don't have to be fumbling around in the dark, not knowing what the issue is or how to deal with it effectively.

We know that nightmares do not come from God, so it is either an attack of the enemy while you are asleep or something that is in your soul or home that gives the enemy legal entrance.

Remember that night that Kiera screamed out in fear because there was a snake demon in her bed? After that happened, I did a thorough cleansing of her room. I went through all her toys and threw a lot of them out. After I did that, it didn't happen again.

So, with the Holy Spirit and His leading, go through your whole house and see what items you may have in your house that may be a legal invitation for the enemy. Simultaneously, loose anything from your children's souls that may be affecting them. You will see the attacks stop. You can trust the Holy Spirit to make it clear to you what you need to do. You are your children's covering. God will speak to you about them.

Chapter 5
Seek God for His Direction for Your Children

The enemy doesn't take it easy on your kids just because they're kids. He is ruthless. He does not even pity babies in the womb. Therefore, we must be vigilant to guard and watch over our children daily.

What does this look like? To begin with, lots of prayer and lots of guidance from the Holy Spirit.

I have chosen to yield to the Holy Spirit since my oldest two children were very young. Although I have not always done this perfectly, my heart was to seek God's will for my life and then obey Him in that which He said. I spent time with the Lord daily and listened to what He would speak to me regarding my children and life choices in general. I do something that I call 'journaling' where I get quiet and tune into the voice of the Lord and just write what I hear the Lord say to me. This is one way that the Lord has been able to speak to me. He also speaks in many other ways.

One day, when I was journaling, the Lord asked me to homeschool my kids. I knew nothing about homeschooling. I grew up in Australia, where it was so rare that I only heard of it one time when I was in the seventh grade because one of my classmates told me that she would be leaving school soon. So I asked her which school she would be going to. She replied, "I am not going to another school; I am going to be homeschooled." I replied incredulously, "You can do that?!"

So, I didn't know anything about homeschooling, but I said in my heart, "Yes, Lord." I let my husband know about what the Lord had said, and originally, he was opposed to it. I didn't worry about it. I just said to the Lord, "Lord, if You want me to homeschool, then you will change Will's heart." The Lord knows that both of us have to be in agreement for me to be able to carry out His word. Over the next few days, the Lord spoke to Will and calmed all his fears about homeschooling. Will then came into agreement that we should homeschool.

I am sharing this word from the Lord about homeschooling because it was one of the many directions that the Lord gave us for our family and for our children. I am not saying that you need to homeschool your children to fulfill God's will for their lives. I am saying that you need to hear God for *your own* children every step of the way.

I know that for us, the decision to homeschool has definitely been a blessing in our lives. We have moved many times since we started schooling the children - eight times to be exact. This includes four times internationally and three times interstate. It would have caused an upheaval in our children's lives if I had to find a new school for them every time we moved. But since we take the school with us wherever we go, it gives them stability.

Homeschooling is also a huge factor in the character development of our children. I am able to disciple them. I don't have to trust a school teacher to raise them up in the fear and admonition of the Lord. Even if there was a teacher who knew and loved the Lord, the laws of the land may prevent them from really being able to teach them the things of God like I am able to.

Since we homeschool our kids, I can choose the curriculum they learn and can decide on a curriculum that honors God and doesn't teach unbiblical content. I can watch over their hearts and their character while they are in their formative years. By the time children are only seven years old, their character and personalities are largely established. Aristotle, the Greek philosopher, put it this way, "Give me a child until he is seven, and I will show you the man."

It is so important that godly mothers and fathers are the primary voices in their children's lives. When we send our kids to daycare and then to preschool and to school, we allow other voices to largely determine what our children will learn, and all of your children's interactions and character development happen largely without you. Therefore, it is so important that you seek the Lord about whether or not He wants you to homeschool your kids, and if not, specifically which school He wants you to enroll your kids into. It's too important a decision to make without the counsel of the Lord.

The Lord told my husband and me to homeschool, and I see His wisdom behind it for our family. At the time He told me, though, I had no idea about all the wonderful benefits. And the beautiful thing is that you don't need to know everything ahead of time. All you need to do is trust and obey Him, and you will see the fruits in due time.

I have a friend who used to be a cosmetologist and who has super adorable 2-year-old twin daughters. She shared with me how the Lord encouraged her to homeschool her children when they come of age. I wanted to share with you what she shared with me. The following is her testimony in her own words:

A Cosmetologists Testimony

Before I was a stay-at-home mother, I was a Cosmetologist. God used this opportunity to not only bring me my husband but to show me that homeschooling my future children was the path that he wanted for me. He brought this knowledge to me with many examples. He showed me the differences between the children who are being homeschooled and the children who are in

Public School. I got to the point where I could mostly point out the homeschooled children as soon as they walked in the door.

I had the sweetest little boy come into my Salon. He was about eight years old. He sat in my chair and carried on the most pleasant conversation with me. In our conversation, I found out that he was homeschooled. I asked him what his favorite class was. I thought that he would either say Math, Science, or Art. But instead, he told me that his favorite class was learning to play the Clarinet. And this was at only eight years old! He wasn't limited by what a school would offer him at the age. And the way he talked about learning to play it and the confidence he had because of this was so pure.

Another time, we had a family of four in our waiting room: A mother with her baby in a carrier, a three-year-old, and a young man probably around the age of twelve. While the mother was getting her baby and toddler settled, her twelve-year-old son walked up to the counter and checked his family in. He knew all of the account information and was very kind and patient. This stood out to me because it was midday, and none of the children were sick. I noted this because a lot of parents bring in their sick children to get haircuts while they are home from public school. The young man impressed me because he had the confidence and the forethought to check his family into the Salon because his mother was busy. Most children his age (I'm using the word children on purpose) would not have done this. The mother would have had to beg and plead for them to do it and end up getting further behind in line and eventually having to do it themselves. I wasn't surprised to learn that these children were indeed homeschooled.

After many years of working in a family-style Salon, I have seen it all. I have witnessed girls from the ages of eight to sixteen wearing clothes that are sexually suggestive, if not completely revealing their bodies. They would wear clothing that was too tight or too short and just not age-appropriate. Their hair was almost always colored with highlights or colored a shade much darker or lighter than the color that God gave them. Now, I have no issues with someone coloring their hair. However, I believe that certain ages are too young for a chemical change in hair. I believe that you should help give your child the confidence to love the way that the Lord made them before allowing them to change their appearance.

That being said. You can tell the difference between a homeschooled child versus one that isn't. Homeschooled children generally dress age-appropriately, and they are confident in their appearance. I believe this is because they don't have the pressure to look like a Hollywood celebrity, or as the girls in the grades above them. They don't have that focus, and instead, their parents are building up their confidence in the Lord and showing them that they are wonderfully made in His image. (Psalm 139:14 and Genesis 1:27)

For example, I once had a homeschooling family in our Salon's waiting room. The ten-year-old girl was wearing a sundress and rain boots while reading her book and patiently waiting for her appointment. The girl on the other side of the room, however, was exactly what I described earlier. She was consumed with her phone and being disrespectful to her mother because she didn't want to get a haircut. She did not appreciate the money or the time her mother was taking to have this done for her. In my years of working at that Salon, God has shown me many comparisons between homeschooling families and families who send their children to public schools. He showed me the stark difference that homeschooling your child makes.

More Eye-Opening Observations

I had the pleasure of cutting another homeschooled child's hair. He was thirteen years old, and he enjoyed skateboarding on his days off. One question that I always found myself asking the homeschooled children was, which of their parents taught them. When I asked this particular boy this question, I was intrigued to find out that neither of his parents taught him. He told me that they both worked full-time jobs. So, instead, he attended Co-op groups for three days a week, and since both of his parents were busy, it worked with their schedules. Then, on their days off, they could spend time as a family. This was God showing me that even *if my future husband and I had to both work full time, I could still give them the education He wanted for them.*

(A Co-op is a group of homeschooling families that get together and share their knowledge of certain subjects with the group. For instance, you may not be great at teaching math and don't feel confident teaching your child, but in the co-op group, there could be another mother who is great at it. So, she would volunteer her time to teach a math class that your child can attend. Conversely, you may be great at photography, science, or cooking. So, you would then teach a class on one of those subjects where the other children of the co-op can attend. It is normally a shared endeavor.)

One day my husband came home from work and was telling me about how he met a couple and that they shared with him that their sixteen-year-old daughter, who had been homeschooled, was attending college because she had already finished her High School education. She was on track to finish her four-year degree by the age of twenty! My husband said he wanted our girls to have that opportunity, the Lord willing. This showed me that not only do homeschooled children have an advantage in character development, they can also be advanced academically.

The Lord also showed me that homeschooled children were more confident. They didn't have to fit in the box that a traditional school provided for them. They could still be very socialized within their churches, sports, or music lessons. The children are much more comfortable around adults and can carry on a conversation even at a young age. They understand and respect what it takes to run a household successfully. They show responsibility for their siblings and themselves. The children are generally very well-rounded and have the opportunity and time to learn the things that interest and inspire them.

The last thing that the Lord taught me about homeschooling was during a time when I had multiple knee operations as a child. During this time, I could not attend school and was instead taught by a teacher who was sent to my home. This teacher would visit my home three to four days a week, and she would stay and teach me for about two to three hours a day. My mother asked her why she was only coming a few days a week and only staying for a few hours since normally school is five days a week, and about seven hours each day. The teacher explained that when you take into consideration things such as your lunchtime, recess, gym time, the time that it takes to come and go to class, and the time it takes for the teachers to deal with the other students, etc., out of the entire day, you may receive only two or three hours of actual learning time. This really opened my eyes to how homeschooling is something that I could do. I don't have to set up my home and follow the same schedule as a public school. Homeschool is more like a tutoring session and can be done in a relatively short time.

I can attest to this. A day of homeschooling can be completed before noon, which leaves the rest of the day to do whatever you want. And as you can see, if you work full-time, there are other options available to you. For example, when we lived in Louisiana, I often took my daughter to the Audiologist because she needed a Hearing Aid for her right ear. I found out that the Audiologist, who was a woman, brought her children to work with her every day. She had a spare room in her office, and she hired a teacher to come for a few hours each day and teach her kids. The room was set up like a classroom with games, books, tables, and chairs. I just thought that that was the coolest thing!

So, as you can see, if the Lord asks you to homeschool your kids, just ask Him how. There are many ways that it can be done.

Homeschooling really was key for me to usher my children into encountering God. Because my children are always around me, I am able to disciple them and pour into them what the Word of God says while also molding their character.

I went to public and private school for fifteen years altogether, and when I really pursued the things of God, it took Him years to get the world's way of thinking out of me and teach me to think according to His Word. It will be very different for my kids. As soon as they complete homeschooling, He will be able to point them in the direction they are to go without having to spend years discipling them beforehand.

My pastor, while I was in Australia this last time, gave me a prophecy while we were getting Judah (our fifth-born) dedicated to the Lord. He said, "Your children are like arrows in the hand of the Lord, and when they are of age, He will pull them back in His bow and shoot them straight into their destinies."

The same will be true for your children as you follow the leading of the Holy Spirit with boldness and turn your back on the world and the way that the world does things.

You can trust the Lord and what He leads you to do with your kids. He loves them even more than you do.

Guarding the Hearts of Your Children

I talk more in-depth about this in my first book, Raising Happy Hearts. Yet, I want to briefly touch on how important it is to guard the hearts of our children. I am sure that you are aware of the battle that is going on in this world to influence your kids. The school curriculum these days is moving further and further away from the truths of God's Word, and they are now pushing openly diabolical agendas. It is so imperative that we protect our children from those ungodly influences as much as possible.

People may say, "You're just coddling your child. They won't be ready for the real world if you protect them so much." "You need to toughen them up."

If you allow the Holy Spirit to lead you in this, you won't hinder the growth of your child. You will only give them room to really blossom.

Adults who have been through really rough upbringings may look tough on the outside, but they are wounded on the inside and often cannot handle the tough situations of life in a wise way. Whereas adults who are whole on the inside and have had a healthy upbringing handle these situations much more wisely and effectively.

My children are protected from a lot of the influence that the enemy has, both through homeschooling them (and thus choosing a godly curriculum and discipling them myself) and through limiting what they watch on TV. Yet, age-appropriately I will share with them some of the ways of the world so that they can be aware. I don't leave them clueless. Yet, I share that information as the Holy Spirit leads.

For example, as I go grocery shopping with my teen daughter, I talk to her about the dangers of predators. I don't tell her all what they do in detail, but just enough so that she gets the point. I let her know to follow the peace of God in her heart. I let her know that if she parks somewhere and has a 'check in her spirit' that something is wrong, then move and park somewhere else immediately.

I also am starting to teach her about how to protect her little ones in the future when she gets married and starts her family. I explain to her that she could get an employee to come out to the car with her if she has any red flags that are going up with a certain individual in the grocery store. I also share with her how important it is to be aware of your surroundings and not to turn your back on your little ones. Predators are looking for mothers that are so focused on what they are doing and not paying attention to their kids. I also teach these things to my teen son.

When I take my son to the gas station, I teach him how to refuel the vehicle. Yet I also teach him to keep his 'head on a swivel' which means that he needs to keep looking to his left and to his right and to be aware of what is going on around him.

As my other four little ones grow up, I will share the same types of information with them.

The Bible says to be wise in what is good but innocent in what is evil (Romans 16:19). So, our children will have the wisdom to know that there are dangers out there and to be wise about avoiding them without knowing the details of all the vile things that predators do. In that way, they will be wise about good and innocent about evil.

Tell Your Kids the Truth

I was working at a Phone Center at a ministry, and I took prayer calls and prayed for many people a day. One lady who called in for prayer told me that she homeschooled her two sons, and now that they are adults, they have completely turned away from the Lord. She said that her sons were upset with her. They would tell her things like, "You told us that people didn't have sex before marriage, and that is not true!"

I know that that is not the whole reason that her children have turned away from the Lord, but it played a part. This book, along with my first book, Raising Happy Hearts, contains a lot of what the Lord has shown me on how to raise up your children to know and love the Lord and be launched into their destinies without becoming snared by the enemy.

It is important not to lie to your children. I don't lie to my children about things. I tell them the age-appropriate truth. I let my teenagers know, "Yes, people have sex outside of marriage, but it is not a good thing." And then I explain to them God's plan about sex and marriage and how the enemy has warped it. Then they understand the truth about it, and they can then make an informed decision to do things God's way and not open up doors for the enemy.

I also don't lie about Santa, the Easter Bunny, or the Tooth Fairy. I don't want them to know that I lie about things and then not believe me about the truth I share about Jesus.

And as for things such as telling them about sex. My children are homeschooled, and so I share it with them when the Holy Spirit leads and not before they are ready.

When they are little and too young to know, I don't tell them that the storks bring them or that they are found in the cabbage patch. I just say things like, "The seed comes from the daddy, and the baby grows in mommy." In my experience, they are happy with that answer. If they were to pry some more, I would simply tell them that I would let them know more when they are older.

The main thing is to be led by the Holy Spirit in all your decisions and never be led by fear. If you have fear about something, rebuke that fear and spend time with the Lord until you are back in peace before you impart to your children. Remember, He is always greater than the enemy, and He is our ever-present help in time of need.

As I have said before, when I was in school, I felt like God was far away, and He wasn't involved in my everyday life. The environment at school and the curriculum didn't help. When I went to do grades eleven and twelve again at a Private Christian School, it was much better, but the damage had already been done. The Lord had to spend years teaching me and training me to walk in His grace and to understand His Word.

However, my ceiling will be my children's floor. They are walking in things of the Spirit that I *still* haven't experienced. By the time they are my age, I can only imagine what they will be doing for the Lord and how close they will be to Him.

The Prophet, Samuel

The prophet Samuel was the last Judge of Israel, and he was the one to anoint Saul and David as kings over Israel. He followed the Lord faithfully his whole life, and he was the one whom God spoke to audibly when he was around eleven years old and living with Eli in the Temple in Shiloh. (Read his story in 1 Samuel 3) Samuel was powerful in Israel and was so in-tune with the Lord and what He was saying to His people, Israel. And before you say, "Oh, but that is Samuel in the Bible, we can't compare to him." Let me just share with you the words of Jesus in Luke 7:28, "Assuredly, I say to you, among those born of women there has not risen one greater than John the Baptist; but he who is least in the kingdom of heaven is greater than he." Therefore, our children and ourselves are greater than Samuel - Jesus, Himself, said so.

Samuel was raised in the Temple, and because of this, he was raised in both the atmosphere and the presence of God. He was also sheltered from so much of the rest of the world and all of its influences. Due to this, he was raised separately from the world.

We also need to live set-apart lives and make an environment for our children where they can live set-apart lives also. The Bible says in 2 Corinthians 6:17, "Come out from among them and be separate, says the Lord."

It's not a bad thing to be separate from the world and not to know about the current social trends and it-people. When I was first pressing into God, I would only use the TV and the internet to watch Christian teachings and Christian content, and I would only listen to Christian worship music. After a while, I realized that I didn't know a lot of the famous people that everyone else knew. I didn't know all the new songs they talked about, and I wasn't aware of all the latest trends. It was a weird feeling at first, but then I realized that I was focusing on what mattered. When I get to Heaven, the Lord isn't going to care about how much of the world I was submersed in. He will be interested in how closely I followed the leading of the Holy Spirit, how much I laid my life down for Him, how well I loved others, and so forth.

It is the same thing with my kids. I realize that they are not like most of the other children. And that's okay. My kids aren't focused on being lustful after celebrities, wearing the latest clothing trends to make sure they look 'cool,' or even focusing on the 'likes' and 'follows' on social media. They are focused on important and eternal things such as hearing what the Lord is saying to them, cultivating their God-given giftings, and being a blessing to the people they interact with. I hear this in their conversations with me, and I see them do this day to day.

I always say to my kids, "If you do what everyone else does, then you get the results that everyone else gets." If you want your kids to be just like everyone else, then, by all means, you don't have to go against the flow of the world. But if you want your kids to be extraordinary and do great things for God, then you need to ask the Holy Spirit to lead and guide you and help you create an environment where He can be the greatest influence in your child's life. It will only bear great fruit.

Chapter 6
Seek God for the Big and the Little Things

We all know that it is important to seek God for the big decisions in life, yet it is also important to seek Him in all the little things. Day to day life is going to bring challenges, and the enemy is always out to steal, kill, and destroy. The enemy tries to put ideas into our children's heads and wants to encourage them to do the wrong things. So, we need to be proactive. We need to be praying for a covering of protection over our children daily.

This is the prayer that I pray over myself, my husband, and our kids in the mornings, "Heavenly Father, I ask You for and receive Your grace for this day. I take authority over this day, and I give it to You to have Your will and Your way in my life, and in the lives of my husband and children. And right now, I take power and authority over all the power of the enemy, and I cancel all of the enemy's assignments against myself and my family right now in Jesus' name. And I command the Host of Heaven to war on our behalf and to tear down any and all strongholds, plots, and plans of the enemy right now. In Jesus' name, you go!"

Here are the Scriptures that I stand on for the aforementioned prayer:

Our authority against the enemy: Luke 10:19, "Behold, I give you the authority to trample on serpents and scorpions, and over *all the power of the enemy*, and nothing shall by any means hurt you." (Emphasis, mine)

Using the Host of Heaven (Heaven's Army) to pull down strongholds and plans of the enemy:

2 Corinthians 10:4-5, "For the weapons of our warfare *are* not carnal but mighty in God for pulling down strongholds, casting down arguments and every high thing that exalts itself against the knowledge of God, bringing every thought into captivity to the obedience of Christ."

Matthew 26:53, "Or do you think that I cannot now pray to My Father, and He will provide Me with more than twelve legions of angels?"

Praying for God's grace for each day: Hebrews 4:16, "Let us, therefore, come boldly to the throne of grace, that we may obtain mercy and find grace to help in time of need."

I also pray in tongues under my breath throughout the day as I am going about my day. I am actually praying in tongues right now as I am writing this book. I do this because praying in tongues allows the Holy Spirit to pray perfect prayers to the Father on your behalf. The Holy Spirit also knows all of the plans of the enemy and can thwart them before they can even manifest in the natural realm. Be on the offensive for your family. It is much better to cover everyone in prayer than to pray to God for help once the enemy has reared his ugly head and caused an issue in your family, finances, health, etc.

In 1 Corinthians 14:18, Paul said, "I thank my God I speak with tongues more than you all." And Paul wrote about a third of the New Testament. Praying in tongues is powerful for more than being on the offensive against the enemy. It can also help us to grow in many other ways as a Believer in Christ.

Here are two more Scriptures about the benefits of praying in tongues: 1 Corinthians 14:4 states, "He who speaks in a tongue edifies himself," and Jude 20 states, "But you, beloved, building yourselves up on your most holy faith, praying in the Holy Spirit."

In this chapter, I have shown you some ways that you can protect your children from the wiles of the enemy. Listening and obeying God and being vigilant in prayer is so key to protecting your children. You need to be willing and obedient in what God asks you to do. God loves your children more than you love them, and He sees the end from the beginning. He already knows what actions will bring about a blessing in your lives and which will not. He always has good things planned for you - much better things than you even have planned for yourself. So, you can trust Him.

If He asks you to do something that you think will be too hard, just know that He will *always* either send you help or give you the grace to do it. For example, if the Lord asks you to homeschool, He is only asking you to do that because you *can* do it and He is right by your side to help. If God asks you to put your kids in a certain school, then He will give you favor so that your child will get accepted into that school.

I know that God is faithful. Every time He has asked us to do something, He has always given us the grace to do it, and He has always sent us the help and the funds we needed to do it. For example, twice He has asked us to move halfway across the world - from the United States to Australia, and then sixteen months later, from Australia back to the United States. Both times we didn't have the money in the natural to even move around the corner! Yet, God *supernaturally* provided for our large family to move internationally *twice*! (This does not include the two times that I went to and from Australia with Kiera, Jerome, and Grace while Will was deployed. Yet, He provided for those flights also.)

As you can see, I live this life of supernatural provision. I am not just giving you lip service. I know from experience that when God asks you to do something, He has already paved the way for you. Just ask Him, "Lord, how did you want me to do this? What is Your instruction?" He not only has a *will*, but He also has a *way*. You need to seek Him for both. He doesn't always do the same thing the same way. He's a creative God.

Seek God for His Way

The first time we moved internationally, God instructed us to contact two like-minded people to pray over us to make the move, and one of them felt led by God to give the exact dollar amount that we needed to fly our then family of six to Australia via a commercial airline. Let's name the lady who donated, Sally. We had no idea that Sally and her daughters would be the ones whom God would choose to provide for our flight. We just called her to let her know what God had asked us to do, and also to ask her to be praying for us. Sally was only one of a couple of people that we know have made big international moves by the Lord's direction. Sally told us on the phone that she and her daughters felt led to give us some money for our flight. We assumed that it would be about $300. It would've been a blessing, but it wouldn't have been a drop in the bucket with what we needed to buy six flights from North Carolina, United States (where we lived at the time) to Sydney, Australia. Yet, we appreciated it regardless. Later on, she told us that her daughters and herself had gathered $6,000 to give to us for our flight! We were amazed! Sally then went on to let us know that when she came to visit us a few months earlier, she saw the number $6,000 appear in the spirit above our heads. She knew that that was the amount we needed to get to Australia. She didn't tell us that at the time; she just began to pray for the Lord to get that money to us. Then the Lord put on her heart to be the one to bless us with that $6,000, along with her daughters.

It was amazing to us! We began to look for flights. I found a flight that we didn't have peace about because it went through a country that we didn't feel was safe, and there was a 24-hour layover there. It was the only flight that cost under $6,000 for all of us. There was one flight that we *did* have peace about. But it cost about $400 more than the $6,000. I originally thought that that flight couldn't be God because it cost more than the amount that He said that we would need. But after much deliberation, we decided that paying only $400 out-of-pocket for a flight for a family of six (at the time) would still be a great testimony to God's provision.

We booked the flights, and there were some hiccups. I accidentally put my married name on the itinerary instead of my maiden name, which was still on my Australian passport. (The Australian Government requires you to have proof of living in Australia for 3 full years after you're married to be able to change your maiden name to your married name on your passport. I hadn't lived in Australia for three consecutive years since I married Will back in 2003. For the majority of our marriage, we have been living somewhere in the United States.) Therefore, I had to call the airline and make the adjustment. We got ahold of an employee of the airline named Greg. The money that we paid for the flight needed to be put back on my debit card again before they could run my card through again. We had to wait for the whole weekend. Greg promised to hold our flight for us while we were waiting. We called back and forth during this process, and then we called on an evening when Greg wasn't at work. We got ahold of another employee. I gave him our itinerary number, and then he told us that we had been bumped off the original flight and had to book another flight a week later. He also said that the price had also gone up from the price we were originally quoted. I got off the phone and felt deflated. I went and talked to my husband about it, and we decided to trust God in spite of it. We got our kids out of their beds and worshipped and praised God together as a family. We went to sleep in peace, and I decided that I would call Greg in the morning.

The morning came and Greg called me before I even had a chance to call him. Greg cheerfully informed me, "Okay, everything has gone through, and I have got you all booked on the flight." I was confused. I asked him which flight he was talking about. He told me that we were booked on the original flight. I was amazed! Then I asked him if the price was still the same. He responded, "Well, I don't know what happened.... but the price decreased to exactly $6,000."

I exclaimed, "I know what happened! Praise God!"

God Moved us Again

After we had been in Australia for 16 months and had our fifth child, the Lord told us to move back to the United States to go to Colorado for Bible College. I sought Him for the way that He wanted us to get there. This time He told us to take a military flight. The military flight was available to us because my husband was retired from the military. These military flights were available to us on the way *to* Australia too, but it is very risky for a family the size of ours because nothing is certain, and we could've gotten bumped off the flight at any stopover along the way and found ourselves stranded somewhere in the world with five kids! The military flights (called Space Available Flights) work kind of like the stand-by flights that family members of employees of commercial airlines get access to. But, since there were seven people in our family at that time, and my husband was retired and not 'Active Duty' in the military, we were the lowest priority to get on a flight. So, not only did we need to get accepted onto a flight, but we also needed seven seats! And we also had to completely move out of our home in Australia in the *hope* that we would be allowed to get on the flight that left *the very next day!!* The US military couldn't confirm that we could get on the flight until the day before it left. Phew! It was such a faith walk! Yet, at the Lord's word, we obeyed Him. The flight left the day after we handed in our keys to our rental home. It left Australia and then had stopovers in Guam and Hawaii before completing the last leg to California. From California, we planned to drive the rest of the way to Colorado. There were miracles and favor along the way, too.

Apparently, I was meant to get permission from the United States Immigration Agency to leave the United States if I planned to be gone from the United States for a period of longer than one year. This was because I was still a Permanent Resident of the United States at the time. I wasn't aware of that rule. When the first leg of the flight was completed, we landed in Guam. Since Guam is an unincorporated territory of the United States, a US Customs and Border Patrol agent checked our passports at the gate. They noticed that I had forfeited my Permanent Residency. As the officer left us at the gate and returned to his office to see what he was going to do with me, Will and I prayed in tongues and believed God for His favor in the situation. We knew that returning to Australia wasn't an option; We had already given away all of our furniture and belongings and had turned in the keys to our home. We had everything we owned packed into suitcases that we brought on the plane with us. We didn't even have money for the return flight home! It was an intense test of faith!

As I am recalling this memory, it reminds me of the Scripture Mark 4:35-41, "On the same day, when evening had come, He said to them, "Let us cross over to the other side." Now when they had left the multitude, they took Him along in the boat as He was. And other little boats were also with Him. And a great windstorm arose, and the waves beat into the boat, so that it was already filling. But He was in the stern, asleep on a pillow. And they awoke Him and said to Him, "Teacher, do You not care that we are perishing?" Then He arose and rebuked the wind, and said to the sea, "Peace, be still!" And the wind ceased and there was a great calm. But He said to them, "Why are you so fearful? How *is it* that you have no faith?" And they feared exceedingly, and said to one another, "Who can this be, that even the wind and the sea obey Him!"

Jesus only did what He saw the Father do, according to John 5:19. Therefore, He saw His Father go to the other side of the sea and obeyed and did likewise. He fell asleep in the boat because He knew He would get to the other side. The disciples, however, looked at the wind and the waves and it rocked their faith. They lost all hope and instead believed that they were about to die.

In both of my testimonies, you can see that even though we got a clear word from the Lord to "go to the other side....of the world.." there were still 'wind' and 'waves' that arose and threatened to stop us from getting to the other side. But we kept the faith and believed God that He would get us to the other side in spite of the obstacles we faced. And He did. He is so faithful.

The Story Continues

After what seemed like a long wait, the officer came back with a form that was filled out. This form waived the requirement that I had just transgressed and allowed me to get back on the flight and continue on to the Continental United States as a US Permanent Resident, without any penalty. Phew! He also waived the fee! Praise God!

The Guam airport was full of people, and many others joined us on our second leg from Guam to Hawaii. (On the first leg, we were the only people on the flight from Australia to Guam other than the crew.) A lot of cargo was also loaded onto the plane. It was a C-17 Globemaster III. The cargo was loaded up in the middle of the plane, and the passengers sat in two single rows along both sides of the aircraft on seats that faced inwards.

We finished the second leg and disembarked in Hawaii for an overnight layover. We also received so much favor there. The airport was packed with people trying to take a military flight back to the continental United States. They weren't allowed to lay down and sleep. They were propped up on walls and pillars, trying to get some sleep. Someone at the airport saw us sitting in the food court with all of our kids and luggage and ushered us into a private room for families that was only accessible with a code. We now had a place to wait overnight with our kids in relative comfort. There was a private room with a TV, kitchen, outdoor playground, and a nursery with a comfortable couch and many baby cribs for our children. This was a blessing because our three youngest were three years, two years, and eleven months old at the time. We were the only family in there for most of the time.

While we were waiting, my husband went to see if we could possibly get onto an earlier flight rather than wait overnight for our flight to take off to California. The lady was so kind. She said that she could put us on a waiting list for a different flight if that's what we really wanted. But then she explained, "The crew has listed your family on the flight's manifest as cargo. You have no danger of being bumped off. Look around at the hundreds of people waiting to get on a flight. If I take you off that flight, you will never get out of Hawaii." Wow! Look at God! It was total favor that He did that for us. It was so unusual. I am glad that my husband went to ask what he asked, so we could see how securely God made a way for us to get to the United States. He's so faithful!

Besides all that favor and perfect timing, it also didn't cost us a thing! The military flight was free for all of us. Before I left Australia, I also felt led to set up an online account for anyone who felt led to sow into our journey. Only one person donated. They donated $1,000. That was enough money for us to hire the vehicle and pay for the gas to make the 20-hour journey from California to Colorado! Therefore, the entire journey was completely free for us! Hallelujah!

When Will and I met, we were both in agreement on having a large family. Will has always wanted six kids, and I came into agreement with him about it. One day, when we already had four kids, I was contemplating life. I was thinking that it would be better to stop at the four kids that we already had instead of having two more. I thought that it would be wiser to stop at four because the more children we had, the harder it would be to travel in between the United States and Australia due to the large expense. I heard the voice of the Lord very clearly. He interjected my thoughts and said to me, "If that's the only reason you want to stop at four, it's not a good reason because I will always provide for you." So, as you can see, He performed what He had promised. Both of the previous testimonies happened after He spoke this to me. I just wanted to share this to encourage you that if the Lord is putting on your heart to have more children, He will not only give you the grace to do it, but He will also supply all your needs. He has always done that with us.

Chapter 7
Practical Ways to Encourage Children to Know the Lord

The most important truth I can share with you that will help your children to love the Lord - and as they grow into adulthood continue to love the Lord - is to instill into them that God is a good God.

The Bible says in Romans 2:4 that it's the *goodness of God* that leads men to repentance.

I know I have mentioned this before in this book, but it bears repeating.

God is a God that leaves the ninety-nine sheep in the pasture to search for the one and rejoices exceedingly when He finds the one. He is the God who sacrificed Himself and took all of the wrath and punishment that we deserve onto Himself so that we would be spared. He is the God Who loves us so much that He numbers the very hairs on our heads and knows us by name.

The Bible even says, in Psalm 139:17-18 TPT, "Every single moment you are thinking of me! How precious and wonderful to consider that you cherish me constantly in your every thought! O God, your desires toward me are more than the grains of sand on every shore! When I awake each morning, you're still with me."

God is constantly, every moment, thinking of us individually. How wonderful is that?

Through our daily life, our actions, and our words, as we show our kids how beautiful, wonderful, kind, and compassionate our Heavenly Father is towards us, they won't run to the world.

My fifteen-year-old son, Jerome, says to me, "Mom, why would anyone even want the things of the enemy when they can have God? I don't understand it!"

Yes, you can raise your kids in such a way that they love God so much and don't want a thing to do with the enemy and his stuff.

God is a Personal God

Last night, Will, the kids, and I had a movie night and we were watching Avatar. There was a part in the movie where the hero, Jake, went to a tree that connected him to their deity. Jake was about to lead his people in a battle against their enemy and was appealing to their god to help them win. Another character in the film is then seen behind him as he is imploring their god for help. She explains to him, "Our great mother does not take sides, Jake. She only protects the balance of life."

When she said this, it annoyed me. Their god was so impersonal and couldn't care less about their lives or anything that they cared about! It then made me even more appreciative of the One True God that we call our God. He is a very personal God. He knows each of us by name, and He fights for us. He laid down His life and defeated hell and the grave just so He could have a relationship with us!

Think about this. Before you were born onto the earth, you were a thought in your Heavenly Father's mind. He decided what you were going to look like, what gifts and talents you were going to have, where and to whom you would be born, and what your destiny was going to be on the earth. He wrote *every day* of your life in His book before any one of them came to be. He then created your little spirit being. When it was time for you to be born on the earth, he knit you together in your mother's womb. (Psalm 139:13). This means that He knit your spirit to the dot of flesh at the very moment of conception. Then, He also assigned an angel to guard over you every day of your life until you returned back home to Him.

What a loving, affectionate, caring, purposeful and amazing God we serve!

Psalm 139:16-18 says, "Your eyes saw my substance, being yet unformed. And in Your book they all were written, The days fashioned for me when *as yet there were* none of them. How precious also are Your thoughts to me, O God! How great is the sum of them! *If* I should count them, they would be more in number than the sand."

Fall in Love with the Lord

So, what is the best way to truly convey to our children how good God is?

It's simple. As *you* fall in love with the Lord, it overflows into the lives of your children. As God shows you how much He loves you through His Word and his acts of love, it then overflows from you and onto your children.

I am always saying, "Hey, kids, gather around! Come and hear what the Lord has done!" And the kids come and hear my testimonies of His goodness, and they rejoice with me.

Also, when my kids get a blessing in their lives, I am quick to bring their attention to the fact that it was God Who did that in their lives. How do I know it was God? It is because the thief comes *only* to steal, kill, and destroy, but Jesus came so that we could have life and that we may have it more abundantly (John 10:10). If it is good, it is God, and if it is not good, it's the enemy.

I teach my kids that God sees what they do in secret, and He will reward them openly, according to Matthew 6:4. I teach them that as they serve willingly, especially without having to be told, and do their work with excellence, the Lord, Himself, will reward them. And I have seen God do that over and over again in my children's lives.

He has blessed them with things and opportunities and experiences and favor that I wasn't able to give to them.

For instance, my older two children started helping and showing more initiative around the house when I gave birth to my sixth child. I had had a cesarean section, and I came down with a cold at the same time. I couldn't do everything that I used to do before the baby was born, and my oldest two children, who were eleven and twelve at the time, started to cook and clean and take care of the things around the house that I usually did myself.

I started to see that they started to get blessed with things that they weren't blessed with before. For instance, my son wanted a Drone to fly around. Then one day, my husband walked in with two Drones that someone had given him for free! Another time, my sister decided to send over money for a gift for my children, and they were able to get the new gaming console they wanted. We had a friend come over once, and my son commented on how he liked his Nike sneakers. So, our friend gave them to him on the spot and drove home in his socks! That same friend also gave my son the knife set he used when he was a cook in the US Army.

Kiera was saving up for an iPad Pro to use for her creative gift to start learning digital art. The Lord put on the heart of another one of our friends to bless her with a large sum of money to go towards purchasing it, and she was able to afford it. Just yesterday, a student of our flight school saw how hard-working my son, Jerome, is and also understood that Jerome was saving up for an iPad Pro to use for his flight training. He then asked me for permission to pay for half of his brand new iPad Pro!

Last year, my four oldest kids were offered a free flying lesson each and now have half an hour of flight time each. Recently, a lady at church handed me two iPhones to give to Kiera and Jerome. They were a huge upgrade from what they had at the time. Kiera and Jerome were praying for new phones because theirs were so old and slow. It was cool to see the Lord provide for them so well. Now, they have better phones than their dad and me!

My third born, Gracie, saw that her older siblings got all these blessings, and she wanted a piece of the pie too. Then, one day, my oldest two kids went over to our elderly neighbor's home, Ms. Sandy's, to scrape all of the snow off her driveway (which they often did). Gracie started crying. When I asked her why she was crying, she said, "I want to go and help Ms. Sandy too."

She saw how much the oldest two were being blessed, and she wanted to be blessed also.

I now have a culture in my home where my children do all their chores with good attitudes. And a lot of the time, they use their initiative and do things that I never asked them to do, such as making *my* bed when I get up in the morning, cleaning and tidying their rooms without being asked, and various chores around the house that I never asked them to do. Then they wait for me to notice. They love it when I notice these things and thank them for them.

And God is faithful, He always blesses them for their efforts, and they learn that He is a good Father and He delights to give good gifts to His children.

Taste and See That the Lord is Good

The kids not only hear from you that He is a good Father, but they also taste and see that the Lord is good. And now that they see that the Lord is good, they aren't enticed by the things of the enemy.

Once you have established that God is a good God and continue to reinforce that truth in the lives of your children, you can start teaching your children Proverbs 3:4-5, "Trust in the Lord with all your heart, And lean not on your own understanding; In all your ways acknowledge Him, And He shall direct your paths."

As I have shared earlier, I used to see God as One Who was far away and was watching me from a distance and not involved in my everyday life.

I have already told you the story of how the Lord showed me that He was actually very close to me at all times and that He wanted to be involved in my day-to-day life and in all my daily activities.

The Lord wants us to acknowledge Him in *all our ways*. The Lord wants us to include Him in our daily lives. When we wash the dishes, we're talking to God; When we're out and about and taking care of errands, we're talking to God; And when we are upset or frustrated, He wants us to talk to Him. The Lord wants us to teach this to our children. He wants, so earnestly, to have a close relationship with each of our children. The best thing that we can do is to cultivate this close relationship between our children and their Lord.

How do we do that as parents?

I have already mentioned how important it is for *you* to have that flourishing relationship with the Lord first. I have also mentioned how important it is to share with your kids how good God is and back this up with regular testimonies from your own life. These are all vital.

In the rest of this chapter, I will share the many other things that I do to lead my kids into a close relationship with God.

Encouraging My Kids to Pray to God Themselves

My kids sometimes come up to me and let me know what they want, such as a specific toy or game or pet. Instead of telling them "No" or trying to figure out how to get that for them, I tell them to ask God for themselves. I just say, "How about you pray to God and ask Him for it?" They normally agree and leave with a good attitude. That is because they have seen God answer their prayers before, so they have faith that He can get it to them.

You can also offer to pray with them in agreement for what they are asking for. Then, when God makes a way to get that thing to them, you can bring their attention to the fact that it was the Lord Who answered their prayers. This goes way beyond 'stuff' and 'things.' Doing this with your children develops a relationship of trust between your children and their Heavenly Father. They will taste and see that the Lord is good and cares about the small things they desire and blesses them with it. Psalm 116 TLB says, "I love the Lord because he hears my prayers and answers them."

And trust me, God will come through for them. They have childlike faith. They just believe. God has done it for my children over and over and over. He does it for us adults also. The main thing for us is we sometimes don't stay in faith and keep believing. We allow doubt and unbelief to come in and steal the answer from us before it manifests in the natural realm.

For example, last year my family and I moved to Corpus Christi, Texas. It is a city on Corpus Christi Bay, off the Gulf of Mexico. We lived in a house that was only a two-minute walk from the Bay. We lived there for seven months before the Lord strategically moved us to another town in inland Texas, near San Antonio. I am not a big fan of fishing, but it is my husband's passion.

When we first moved to Corpus Christi, my husband went out early in the mornings, and one day he came home with two large Redfish. Redfish are beautiful fish with a black dot on their tails. Then, all of a sudden, a desire rose up within me to catch a Redfish for myself.

I prayed to the Lord, "Lord, can you please bless me to catch a special Redfish?" For some reason, other large fish weren't appealing to me. I wanted the Redfish.

I woke up early to go fishing with my husband - something I *never* thought I would do - and I tried to catch a Redfish. I was unsuccessful. We went morning after morning and also evening after evening. I would catch other small fish, and occasionally my husband would catch more Redfish. I would get disheartened and wonder where my special Redfish was. But I also remembered that my timing is not the Lord's timing. I encouraged myself that the Lord had heard my prayer and that He would answer me. I would thank the Lord in advance. As I would fish, I would say, "Thank You, Lord, for my special Redfish. Thank You that You have heard my prayer and that You have answered me."

Still Awaiting the Answer to My Prayer

Weeks passed, and the days started getting colder, and I stopped fishing. A few months later, we purchased a house near San Antonio and were preparing to move within a few days. Out of the blue, I got a call from Will, and he was super excited. He could see huge schools of large Redfish swimming in the Bay right near our home. I knew that this might be the only chance I had to catch my special Redfish before we moved inland. So I jumped in the car and met my husband at the Sea Wall. He rigged up my Fishing Rod, and I cast out my baited hook with the hope of finally catching my special Redfish. In just a few casts, I hooked onto a giant one! I reeled it up, and I was so excited to see that the Lord had finally blessed me with my special Redfish. It was 28 inches long, and that was the largest it could legally be before we would've had to release it. Wow! I was so blessed.

The Lord used this to confirm to me that He cares about the things that matter to us. He answered my prayer on the first day that I prayed, and He knew that the day would come that I would catch my special Redfish. He also showed me that He blesses us beyond what we ask or even think! After I caught that one Redfish, I caught many, many more. I could've caught one hundred of them if I stayed long enough (and if it were legal, of course). It was such a fun time! In the clear water, we could see the massive school of large Redfish swimming along the Sea Wall, and we would run up and down the Sea Wall, casting into the school and would hook them with almost every cast! Other fishermen saw the success we were having, and my husband showed them all how to rig their own fishing rods to catch their own Redfish. He even gave them his own lures so that they didn't have to leave and buy them themselves. Great sounds of joy were heard up and down the Sea Wall. It was the best time!!

Another thing that He showed me through this is that He gives us the desires of our hearts. Now, that *does* mean that if there's something we desire in our hearts, He gives that thing to us, but it also means that He is the One Who put the very desire in our hearts in the first place! Have you ever thought of that? God is the reason you desire something in the first place. He gives you the desire for something, and then He fills it to make your joy complete.

A Blessing in Hawaii

I believe He wants me to share a second story about this. When I was a little girl in Australia, my biggest dream was to go on vacation to Hawaii. Now, if you live here in America, it may not seem like such a huge deal. But, to a little girl in Australia, it was a big dream!

A couple of years ago, the Lord made a way for my husband and me to vacation in Hawaii. It was the honeymoon that we never had. It was the best time of my life! When we showed up in Honolulu, we went to get a rental car. The lady behind the desk had on a beautiful ring made up of two Tahitian Black Pearls that joined with gold around the back of her finger and were offset. I thought it was a beautiful ring and that it looked stunning on her with her darker Hawaiian skin. We left that place, and I didn't think about it again. I was just enjoying Hawaii. A few days into our trip, we made a road trip up to the North Coast to see Waimea Beach and the sights along the way. We stopped at a Shave Ice Kiosk. (They call it 'Shave Ice' in Hawaii.) The lady behind the counter who was serving us had on the *same ring*! All of a sudden, a desire was birthed in my heart. I wanted that ring before we flew back home.

I told Will about it, and we went on the lookout for one. We looked in many jewelry stores and even the large flea market in Honolulu. I couldn't find that ring. So we tried Walmart, and the jewelry kiosk attendant let us know of a place where we would definitely find the ring.

I was so excited as I pulled up that jeweler's website on my phone. My heart dropped when I saw the price. They were thousands of dollars apiece!

Will and I went back to our Airbnb in Kailua and spoke with our Airbnb Host, who lived in the main house attached to the Airbnb rental. I told her about our unsuccessful search to find one of those elusive Tahitian Black Pearl rings.

Our Airbnb host let us know that she actually was a jewelry maker, and she sold her Hawaiian-themed jewelry on Etsy. She said that she knew where I could get Wholesale Tahitian Pearls at a fraction of the cost. She also said that she knew of a lady who could place those pearls onto a gold band and form them into the exact ring I was after. I was so blown away! I ended up finding a grouping of five beautiful Tahitian Black Pearls wholesale for under $100. The colors of the pearls were a mix of beautiful champagnes, silvers, and bronzes, which worked so well with my skin tone. Then our Airbnb host's friend kindly put four of them into two beautiful rings for only $50. I was so blessed! I had not one but *two* rings worth thousands of dollars made for under $150! I was in awe of God. He gave me the desire just so that He could bless me with two beautiful keepsakes from Hawaii. I wear them to remember our time in Hawaii and the kind act of God.

As you look back on your life, I am sure that you have stories of your own to share. God is faithful! We must encourage our children to ask God for the desires of their hearts so that He can show Himself faithful to them and thus cultivate a close trust relationship with them from an early age.

Encourage Your Kids to Converse with the Lord

Another powerful thing that you can do is to encourage your kids to talk with the Lord throughout the day and to be mindful that He is with them everywhere. Some people call this 'practicing the presence of God'.

God is with us at all times, yet we often don't recall Him to mind. Being mindful of God throughout our day is a powerful thing. It even says In Proverbs 3:6, "In all your ways acknowledge Him, And He shall direct your paths."

I have found that the more things I do that are centered around Him, the easier it is to think about Him and acknowledge Him throughout my day. I have found that when I watch a lot of secular programming and listen to secular songs, that is what is playing in my head all day.

In contrast, if I listen to Christian teaching and worship music, that comes to my mind throughout the day instead. When I wake and spend time with Him first thing in the morning and allow Him to speak to me, then I am meditating on the things that He showed me and spoke to me for the rest of the day. Yesterday, the kids were watching the movie Frozen II. I was sitting on the couch doing my own thing, yet the catchy songs from that movie played through my head, and I started singing them. Then this morning, when I went to spend time with the Lord, I didn't have worship music playing in my head like I normally do; it was Frozen songs instead! Now, this is not a terrible thing or anything. I was just using it as an example of how what you watch or listen to ends up being what you think about.

I tried to 'practice the presence of God' a few years back. At the same time, I was listening to secular music while I was exercising, and I was watching certain programming on YouTube that wasn't a sin, but it wasn't focused on the Lord either. At the time, I wondered why it was so hard to keep my focus on the Lord throughout the day. But, when I made the shift to spending more time doing activities that were God-focused, I had an easier time keeping my mind stayed upon Him.

We can teach this to our kids. We can also create a culture in our home where we talk about the Lord throughout the day. I like to ask my kids, "What has the Lord shown you?" "What has the Lord spoken to you?" When my kids share with me what they think they've seen or heard the Lord say, I encourage them. This is so important. When your kids know that what they're seeing or hearing is from the Lord, it will encourage them to keep going!

I also listen to the kids when they tell me their dreams. Then, I help them to discern whether it was a dream from the Lord and if so, help them with the interpretation.

I also like to put on worship music and Christian teaching. We talk together about testimonies about what the Lord has done, and we include the Lord in our conversations. By this, I mean that we talk about Him almost constantly. The Bible says in Luke 6:45 that from the abundance of the heart, the mouth speaks. So, when we get so full of God, it is inevitably what comes out of our mouths. This is really helpful when we want to impart a love for God and a culture where He is central in the lives of our children.

You can also tell the kids that they can thank Him throughout the day. This also helps to keep their mind stayed on Him. Tell them that when they wake up in the mornings, they can say, "Good morning, Lord. Thank You for this beautiful day. Thank You for my delicious breakfast. Thank You, Lord, for my family." This starts the day on the right foot. You can also ask your kids throughout the day, "What are you thankful to the Lord for?"

For your older children with phones, there are actually apps that you can download onto their phones that send out a reminder as frequently as you would like them to. I downloaded one of these apps, and I set it to remind me to be thankful to the Lord every fifteen minutes throughout the day to begin with. When the reminder would go off every fifteen minutes, I would thank the Lord for at least one thing. I found that my prayers started to be answered in a supernaturally fast way - just from that one discipline. You can try it and see how it changes your life too! You don't have to set the timer that frequently either. You can set it every half an hour, or every hour also.

There are also Bible Apps with reading plans with commentaries that they can follow along with. 'You Version' is my favorite.

Chapter 8
Encourage Your Kids to Spend Time With The Lord

When your kids are older, you can encourage them to start putting aside time to spend some time with the Lord. When Kiera was twelve and Jerome was eleven, I let them know that they can't piggyback off of my relationship with the Lord; they need to cultivate one with Him themselves.

I told them they needed to wake up early and spend time with the Lord before breakfast. So the next morning, they both decided to do that.

The next morning was mind-blowing! We didn't even do our homeschooling because of what happened that next morning. Kiera had a dream of Christ Jesus opening her bedroom door. She was then awoken by the audible Voice of God. It awoke her from her slumber. The Voice said, "Come out here, and I will show you something you've never seen before." She said that when she woke up, her bedroom door was opened even though she had closed it before she went to sleep. She walked out of her room and went to her brother's bed in the next room. Her presence shocked him awake, and he was awakened out of what I can only describe as a night vision about his future. They both come upstairs to tell me what had occurred. Jerome started telling me about what he saw in the future when he and Kiera were grown, and only the four little ones still lived with my husband and me. He told us who Kiera was married to, what his name was, where they lived, what their children's names were, and what genders they were. Kiera just repeatedly gasped, saying, "I never told you that!" Apparently, that was all a confirmation of what the Lord had already shown her. He also shared where my husband and I were living at the time. We were in a whole different state. Wow! I was amazed!

I am continually amazed at how the Lord pursues my kids and how the Holy Spirit teaches them and speaks with them independently of me.

A few years ago, Jerome was cleaning the kitchen because it was his chore for the night. However, he had not done a great job. I was speaking to him about the importance of doing a great job. I let him know how important it was to always do things with excellence because then everyone will know him as a person of excellence. I also mentioned that it is important not to be known for sub-par work and subsequently chip away at his good name. He listened to me, finished his work in the kitchen, and then went upstairs to his room.

Later on, he came downstairs and said to me soberly, "I went upstairs into my room and I started reading Proverbs in the Bible and I realized that what you said to me was true."

I was amazed. What young boy goes upstairs to his room after he is scolded, to read his Bible and meditate on his mother's words? It was wonderful to me that while he was in his room, the Holy Spirit was there with him and spoke to him and confirmed the word of God to him that I had spoken. Wow! So, that's why I want to encourage you that we are co-parenting with God. We are led by the Holy Spirit in how we raise our kids, and we trust the Holy Spirit to do what we cannot. And He is so faithful. He will speak to our kids, minister to them, and even give them revelation. They are not filled with a junior Holy Spirit.

This is probably a great time to point out that we can lead our children in the Sinner's Prayer so that they can receive the Lord for themselves. We can also pray with them to receive the Baptism of the Holy Spirit with the evidence of speaking in tongues. We can also baptize them in water, as the Scriptures instruct.

When our children are filled with the Holy Spirit, He becomes *their* Comforter, Teacher, Counselor, etc. It makes our lives so much easier. And praying in tongues is another thing that we can encourage them to do throughout the day.

What I like to do is to pray in tongues quietly and even sometimes under my breath, all throughout the day. It is a powerful thing to do. When we pray in tongues, we allow the Holy Spirit to pray perfect prayers of faith to our Heavenly Father on our behalf. The Holy Spirit knows our future and prays prayers that help us to fulfill our destinies.

Seeking God Diligently

As I write this chapter, Kiera and Jerome are sixteen and fifteen years old, respectively. I have them get up quite early in the morning to spend time with the Lord before the four little ones get up for the day. All three of us spend a good hour to an hour and a half with the Lord before the day starts. I meet with the Lord in my prayer closet while Kiera and Jerome meet with Him in their bedrooms. I teach them what to do during those times and give them the freedom to be led by the Holy Spirit during their time with the Lord. We do this because we know that the Lord is a rewarder of those that diligently seek Him. (Hebrews 11:6).

As I have pressed into God, I have had more things of the supernatural open up to me. I am hearing Him clearer than ever before, and He has been giving me visions of the future also. The more I experience, the more I am excited to wake up in the morning to spend time with Him.

But it wasn't always like this. Time with the Lord can start out kind of dry. But the more you spend time with Him and the more you diligently seek Him, the more of Him that you get, and the more the things of the supernatural open up to you.

We can encourage our kids with this. As they start spending time with the Lord, it may not be spectacular. Relationships are cultivated with time. However, it may just be spectacular for them. I will share more of my kids' testimonies of their encounters with the Lord in this book.

Here are some things that you can encourage your kids to do during their time with the Lord. They can pray in tongues, read the Bible, read a devotional book, read a Christian teaching book, listen to an online teaching or podcast, or worship with music or without.

They can also get out a notepad and pen and listen for what the Lord is saying to them and write what they hear. They can also sit still before the Lord and wait in stillness with their eyes closed for what the Lord would want to show them. I do this a lot. When I get quiet and just sit still with my eyes closed, I feel the presence of the Lord, and he speaks to me and gives me visions. These visions are just quick pictures that appear seemingly in my imagination. When I see them, I immediately ask the Lord, "What does that mean?" "What do you have to share with me about that?" and then He tells me the meaning of what I just saw.

I encourage my children to do this too. This is called 'waiting on the Lord'.

Teach Your Children the Word of God

It is important to teach your children the Word of God. They need to have a firm foundation of what the Word of God says so that when something is said to them, masquerading as the truth, many Scriptures will come to mind to confirm to them that what they are hearing is against Scripture. Then they can just throw it out like sticks among the hay.

The Bible says in Deuteronomy 6:6-9, "And these words which I command you today shall be in your heart. You shall teach them diligently to your children, and shall talk of them when you sit in your house, when you walk by the way, when you lie down, and when you rise up. You shall bind them as a sign on your hand, and they shall be as frontlets between your eyes. You shall write them on the doorposts of your house and on your gates."

This Scripture talks about the importance of constantly speaking about the Word of God to your children throughout the day. It also talks about writing out the Word and placing it in areas so that your children can see it regularly. You can ask the Holy Spirit to give you ideas on how to do that. The wisdom behind this is that your life moves in the direction of your most dominant thought. If our children are just watching secular TV programs all day, then they will start thinking like the world and have the same results that the world is having. But if they are more focused on the Lord and His Word, then they will have the results that the Bible says that they can have. Remember Samuel in the Temple? Sure, it will take effort. It always takes effort to swim against the stream. But remember why you are wanting to raise kids contrary to the way the world raises kids. You want your kids to know the Lord intimately, to know His voice and obey Him, and to do mighty signs and wonders for Him.

Jesus says in John 14:12, "Most assuredly, I say to you, he who believes in Me, the works that I do he will do also; and greater *works* than these he will do, because I go to My Father."

We won't be able to raise a generation that will do the works of Jesus, and even greater works, if they are fed on a daily diet of whatever the world dishes out.

Another great way to teach your kids the Word of God is to have them read the Word for themselves. This is especially important when they are teenagers. The Word of God is our solid foundation. I would say that most believers have never even read the whole Bible through even one time. It is powerful when you get to read it for yourself and see for yourself what it says.

You can also recommend certain teachers that they can listen to online. I recommend certain teachers to my kids that I have been listening to for years, and I know that they speak the Word of God and I can trust them. One of these people is Andrew Wommack. The Lord led my husband and me to attend his Bible College in Colorado back in 2014. His teaching covers the foundational principles of the faith and will help your children to have a solid foundation on the Word of God. All of his teachings are free on his website www.awmi.net. You can also find him on YouTube. He also has study guides that you can purchase that go along with his teachings. You can use these to lead your children through Bible Studies. There is one in particular called Discipleship Evangelism. It is a study guide that takes a new believer through all the basic doctrines of the Christian faith, such as Eternal Life, Baptism, Integrity of God's Word, The Nature of God, Authority of the Believer, etc. In the Study Guide are questions that you can ask your child, and then it has the answers with corresponding Scripture references. It's a powerful tool.

My daughter, Kiera, has recently been listening to two of Andrew Wommack's teachings throughout the day. She said that when she is working on her digital art, she has one of his teachings playing in the background. She says that she really enjoys his teachings and is learning so much. I can see the fruit of it in her life.

A few times, when I have walked upstairs to their bedrooms at night when the little ones are in bed, I have found Kiera and Jerome listening to one of Andrew Wommack's teachings together.

It blesses me that my teenagers are never a source of grief for me. They continually bless me every day. You also don't need to expect your children to grow into rebellious teenagers. Partner with God in raising them, and you can trust Him for the good fruit to be evident throughout their lives.

Chapter 9
Light a Fire in the Hearts of Your Children

One day recently, I was talking with my older two kids on our back porch. Our light-hearted conversation shifted, as it frequently does, and we started to talk about the deep things of God. When our conversations start to get into the deep things of God, I make it my priority to stay in that place with them and really minister to my children and answer all of their questions. Schoolwork can wait, and chores can wait. Their relationship with the Lord and understanding spiritual truths are the most important things in their lives.

The Lord faithfully led me during that conversation, as He always does, and I started to share with the kids that the things that we do here on earth are rewarded in Heaven, and the more we partner with the Holy Spirit and His grace, the more we will be rewarded in Heaven. I shared that while we are here on this earth, we are qualifying for a position in Heaven.

I shared with them the details of a vision that the Lord had shared with me through a book written by Rick Joyner called, The Final Quest. This vision that Rick had received from the Lord really 'lit a fire under me,' so to speak. And it encouraged me to really pursue God with my whole heart when I was in my early twenties.

In the vision, Rick found himself before the Lord's throne, where there were multitudes of people that extended even further than the eye could see. These were the redeemed of the Lord. The people closest to the throne of God were the ones who lived their lives for Him on earth, and the people who were furthest away from the throne were the foolish ones who got saved and then lived self-centered lives. They are the ones who did what they wanted to do without laying their lives down for Jesus.

He also saw people sitting on beautiful thrones that were a part of God's throne. Many of those thrones were occupied by believers who had already gone to Heaven, but there were still a great many thrones that were vacant and still to be filled by people on the earth. The Lord explained to him that these thrones were for the "Overcomers', The Overcomers were the believers who had served Him faithfully on the earth. These Overcomers were now rulers in Heaven and also of cities on the earth. He saw many great people upon those thrones, people from all walks of life who had been faithful with what they had been given to do. But the largest demographic of people who sat on these thrones were praying women and mothers!

This brought me so much hope! Now I know that as long as I am faithful with what the Lord is leading *me* to do, I will be able to sit on one of those thrones too.

The Scripture confirms this in Revelation 3:21, "To him who overcomes I will grant to sit with Me on My throne, as I also overcame and sat down with My Father on His throne."

As you can see, it does not say that this is for 'he who lives an ungodly life, yet makes a deathbed confession of faith' or for 'he who lives a mostly worldly life and refuses to fully yield to the Spirit'. But it is for 'he who overcomes' - the believers who have served God faithfully on the earth; The ones who laid down their own will and submitted it to the will of the Father. They are the Galatians 2:20 people, "I have been crucified with Christ; it is no longer I who live, but Christ lives in me."

The Stones of Fire

I was also sharing with the kids that another minister, named Kevin Zadai, saw the 'stones of fire' in Heaven spoken about in Ezekiel 28:14 after he died on the operating table. He called them the 'Sapphire Stone'. Jesus explained to him that the only people allowed to step onto the Sapphire Stone in Heaven are those who had cultivated a close relationship with Him on the earth; Not everyone that is saved will be able to step foot onto it. Therefore, there will be people in Heaven for all eternity that will never be allowed to step foot upon it because they weren't focused on their relationship with Jesus while on the earth. Instead, they just wanted 'fire insurance,' so to speak. That is, they received Jesus as their Savior so that they wouldn't have to go to hell but didn't make Him Lord of their lives. There are also others who instead of pursuing God in all holiness and fear of the Lord, try to see how closely they can live in the world yet not miss out on Heaven. These people will not get the privilege that will be awarded to those who pursued Jesus with their whole hearts.

These types of revelations have always lit a fire under me that made me cry, "Lord, I want all that you have for me. I want to do all that You want me to do. Use me in any way that You will. Help me to fulfill my destiny and be as close to you as I possibly can!"

As I shared these things with Kiera and Jerome, it was like a light bulb had gone off. Kiera commented, "Oh! All this time, I thought that I needed to press into God just to get the enemy off my back. I had no idea that there's actually a goal to pursue. I thought that everyone in Heaven got the same thing. Now that I know different, I have a goal to be on one of those thrones." Jerome also felt the same way.

This really lit a fire in them to pursue God with their whole hearts. Jerome tells me that now when he has the choice to watch some entertainment on YouTube or to spend time with the Lord, he asks himself a question. He asks himself, "Do I want to watch this show to be entertained for the moment, or do I want to spend time with God, which will count for eternity?"

Provoking to Jealousy

Here's a funny story. I will preface this by saying that I will share many things that the kids have experienced with the Lord in the next chapter. For many years they have regularly provoked me to jealousy with their awesome encounters. I would always be pursuing God and not even seeing a fraction of what they were seeing.

This morning, Kiera, Jerome, and I were sitting in the living room talking with each other after our individual times of intimacy with the Lord. In the past couple of months, I have been putting more weight on what the Lord has been showing me and have been honoring what I have been seeing. Therefore, I am receiving profound revelations from the Lord and warnings of the future. I have also been hearing the Lord more clearly when He speaks to me. As I was sharing this with Kiera and Jerome, Jerome said to me, "Man, you're making me jealous!" I blurted back to him, "Now you know what it feels like!" We all laughed together.

The Lord will let you know what to share with your kids and when. He is the Vinedresser. He knows when to prune and when to water. He knows when your individual children are ready to receive certain truths and when they are not. He will lead you in this.

And don't be dismayed. You may think, "But I can't hear God that clearly!" Rest assured that you can! You hear Him more than you realize. After what seemed like a dry season in my life, I cried out to God, saying, "Lord, I can't hear you!" Immediately I heard in my heart the voice of God saying, "Yes, you can, because you are obedient to what you hear me say."

I was taken aback. Even though I *thought* that I wasn't hearing God, in reality, I was. I was just not hearing Him the way I was expecting. Most of the time, we mistake God's thoughts for our own thoughts because we have the mind of Christ. (1 Corinthians 2:16). It just takes time to discern the difference.

So, you can motivate your children with your own testimonies of your time with the Lord, and you can share with them certain teachings or ministers that really gave you that desire to press into God.

The Main Thing

The main thing that I need to reiterate in helping your children to pursue an intimate relationship with Jesus, apart from having your own intimate relationship, is telling them and showing them that He is a good God.

You need to know this for yourself first. Ask God to show you His true nature. I can also recommend Andrew Wommack's teaching, 'The True Nature of God,' to help you.

When I was just starting my journey of pressing into God, for years, I had a deep fear that I was going to lose my salvation. I would lie in bed at night and be so afraid that I would end up going to hell. I was living a very holy life, but I was afraid that I would get to the end of my life and get before the judgment seat of God and hear God say, "Well, I *would* let you in, but you didn't do this or that, or you *did* this or that, and I can't let you in."

The enemy would even warp Scripture to confirm my fears.

I remember acting out of that fear. One time, I remember yelling at my little brother while I still lived at home, "Stop doing that! Do you want to go to hell?!?" I was afraid for him too.

Years went by, and one day my father-in-law felt led to share one of Andrew Wommack's teachings with me. It was the teaching named 'Eternal Life' in his Spirit, Soul, and Body series.

Andrew shows, from the Scripture, our security in Christ and how it is *not* as easy as I thought to lose our salvation. This blessed me beyond measure, and I was for once secure in my salvation and filled with joy! That joy has remained.

Now, I don't have that fear to project onto my kids because it's gone. I can speak to my kids from my place of having a close, personal, and *secure* relationship with Christ.

The Lord will also lead you into freedom in any areas that you are bound. Yield to Him and partner with Him, and He will set you completely free.

Chapter 10
My Children's Testimonies

Over the years, my children amaze me with the things they see and experience with the Lord. I want to share a few of them in this chapter.

When Grace, my third-born, was eight years old, she had a dream or vision of our family, and the Body of Christ, in a battle against the enemy. I was amazed at what she said to me. I knew that this dream or vision was directly from the Lord.

In the battle that was taking place in her dream, she saw me. I was blocking every attack of the enemy with my shield and then killing the enemy and advancing. If I saw someone getting attacked, I would go back and rescue them. Gracie said I was so good, and I never got hurt because I had years of experience.

Gracie said that every time she got knocked down, Jesus would come and put His shield over her to protect her. She said that Jesus was with me too, but He didn't need to intervene because I was doing so well.

Gracie said that Will (my husband) was behind me, watching my back, and when demons came to attack me from behind, Will would kill them. She also said that the Body of Christ won the war.

Wow! What a powerful visual of what we do in the Spirit Realm every day. It especially blessed me that she saw my husband, Will, watching my back and taking out the enemy on my behalf. I know he has done this for me our whole marriage. He sees my blind spots and thwarts the plans of the enemy against me. We're a team. I always say that I wouldn't be the woman of God that I am today without him.

A Vision of Heaven

Another time, when Grace was around the same age, she knocked on my bedroom door at night after I had already sent her to bed. I opened the door, and she was standing there crying. I asked her what was wrong, and she started sharing with me what had just happened. She said, with tears streaming down her face the whole time, "When I was praying, I looked 'deeper' with my eyes closed, and then I saw God. He gave me a diamond crown, and He told me that I was a leader. And I saw God and Jesus, and God was so beautiful and so golden and a little bit yellow. And I also saw Heaven, and it was so beautiful and golden. And I saw the rooms that were really nice and clean that you guys will love.

And then I saw a battle between Jesus and the enemy. The enemy was so scary, so God just blinded his face so that I couldn't see it. I knew that whoever won the battle would be the one that I would serve. And Jesus won, and so I was going to serve Him."

I could tell that she had a real encounter. I was blown away when she shared her testimony.

It also made me smile with her descriptions of what she saw.

Grace had another encounter when she was six. She said, "Jesus hugged me so nice, and He kissed me, and He is very nice, and I love Him so much. And He was strong. He was saving me from the water because it hurts. And He loves me so much. He told me to fold the clothes so neatly. He said to put my clothes on one side, and Lily's on the other side, and He said, "Good job" when I was done." To make this story clearer, the encounter she had with Jesus bore good fruit in her life. Later that same day, as she was folding the laundry, she continued to hear from the Lord, and she remained sensitive to His voice and obeyed His voice.

Grace just shared this encounter with me as if it were the most natural thing in the world. I thought it was precious that she described how Jesus hugged and kissed her since her love language is physical touch. So, Jesus showed her love in her love language. Secondly, when she talks about the 'water that hurts', I believe she is talking about the Lake of Fire that the Bible talks about in Revelation 19:20. She had no idea about the Lake of Fire. She was only six at the time.

When Lily, my fourth born, was six, she said to me, "I saw Jesus. He said that you made me kind, and now I am kind."

I thought that that was really cute. Lily has always been such a sweet girl ever since she was a baby. As she got older, every now and again I would notice little things that she would do that were not so sweet. It would've been easy for me to overlook them since she was such a sweet girl. But I decided that I was going to discipline her when she needed it because I wanted her to stay a sweet girl. And so, I did. Then to hear this from her blessed my heart and made me smile.

More Powerful Encounters

About five years ago, Kiera let me know that she had visions of Heaven. She said that she saw my mansion in Heaven, and she described to me what she saw. In my mansion, she saw the baby that I had recently miscarried, and there was a sign above his crib with the name 'Caleb Bellamy' on it. (This made me teary. At the beginning of this pregnancy, when I hadn't realized that I had miscarried, the Lord gave my husband a dream. In the dream, he was shown a grown man who was standing right next to God, Who was sitting on His throne. My husband then knew that I had miscarried and that it was a son. We named him Caleb Andrew.)

She also saw what looked like beautiful tree branches coming down from the ceiling of my mansion. At the end of each branch, crystals were hanging down. Multiple crystals were attached to each branch by a strand. In each crystal was one of my memories from the earth. She said that all I had to do was turn one of the crystals towards myself, and it would replay a precious memory of mine. (This also meant a lot to me because I have very precious memories of my family.)

She also saw a portal in my mansion. Over the portal was written the words: 'Have some fun with Jesus portal.' She said that anytime that I wanted to spend time with Jesus, I just had to walk through that portal. There were also smaller details that she shared with me. Then she illustrated the mansion on four pieces of paper and taped them together into a house shape before putting on a roof. When I was looking at her illustration, I saw that the view out of the window was a mountainous landscape with snow-capped mountains. I asked her why that was the view outside of my mansion. Kiera replied, "God knew that you loved mountains, and so He made some mountains near your mansion for you to look at." She also mentioned that my husband's mansion is right next to mine.

All of this just melted my heart and endeared me to the Lord even more. He really does care about the small things that we care about.

Another prophetic instance happened when Kiera was about eight years old. I was on the phone with my sister, Stephanie, who was living on the island of Samoa at the time and attending Rhema Bible College, South Pacific. I was praying with her because she had just suffered a miscarriage. She already had a son and was believing God to bless her with a daughter. Kiera was not listening to our conversation, but she was at the table drawing a picture. In the picture, she drew Stephanie and her husband. She then drew a baby in Stephanie's tummy and then a girl standing right next to her with long hair and a heart coming out of her head. She explained to me that Stephanie's daughter loves her mom very much. Within a few weeks, my sister conceived her precious daughter, Vivienne. I was amazed at how prophetic her drawing was. I just recently asked Kiera about why she drew that picture. She told me that she just wanted to draw something, and then all of those ideas just popped into her head, and she just drew them. So, she was listening to the Holy Spirit without realizing it and drew a prophetic and comforting drawing for my sister overseas.

When Grace was seven years old, she created a drawing also. It was a drawing of me with a huge belly. Inside my belly were nine babies. I was so amazed. Between the six babies I have given birth to, plus the three I have miscarried, she drew the exact number of pregnancies/babies that had God blessed me with. Wow!

Kiera and Jerome also regularly see the angelic and demonic, and I hear them say things such as "Mom! I just saw a big angel behind you!" Or, they talk about the angels they saw when they went to bed the night before. They also see the demonic and command it to go.

This is another form of motivation that they have to not choose the things of the enemy - They can literally see how bad choices open up doors for him to come in. They can see how important it is to live a holy life and to keep all the doors closed to the enemy.

Voice of Many Waters

I shared earlier in the book that Kiera was woken up by the audible voice of God. She said it sounded like many voices talking at the same time. The Holy Spirit then recalled to my remembrance that Ezekiel described God's voice as the 'sound of many waters' in Ezekiel 43:2. God's voice is layered, and so that is why it can sound like many people talking at the same time.

Another time that Kiera heard the voice of God, it sounded like my voice saying excitedly, "Kiera, look!" She thought it was me, but I was nowhere around.

Grace once came to my bedroom and asked me what I wanted. I told her that I didn't call her. She said that she had heard me call her. We both thought it was strange. However, Grace returned to her room.

Grace then heard my voice calling her a second time, and she came to ask me what I wanted. A second time I had to let her know that it wasn't me who called her. She was confused. I then remembered the story of Samuel in the Bible when the Lord called his name three times, and all three times, he thought that it was Eli calling him. It appears that the voice of God can sound however He wants it to - both the sound of many waters and also the voices of our loved ones. I asked the Lord why He sometimes chooses to sound like me when talking audibly to my children. He told me it was because it was a voice that they are familiar with, and it is a comforting voice to them.

The last testimony that I wanted to share is about the cover of this book. I had a thought one day, "Wouldn't it be cool if Kiera could illustrate the cover of this book?" I asked Kiera if she wouldn't mind doing that for me. She was nervous and unsure of herself, but she accepted. One morning, Kiera was awoken, and the Lord gave her the vision for the cover of this book. As you can see, it depicts a mother with her daughter. The mother is looking at the natural realm, but her daughter is looking beyond the natural and can *also* see into the unseen, or spirit realm. How powerful is that? The Lord Himself gave my daughter a vision of what this book's cover should be. Not only that, the vision perfectly portrays the whole theme of this book. It just warms my heart.

So, as you can see, your children don't have a junior Holy Spirit. They can have powerful encounters with the Lord and see into the spirit realm a lot more easily because they are not so blinded by this world. I always get so amazed at how the Lord speaks directly to them and gives them encounters with Him that are independent of anything I had to do for them to encounter Him. My children are His children first, and He wants to speak with them and lead and guide them personally, just like He does with us.

There have been times when the Lord has brought conviction to them or given them ideas on what to do to be a blessing to myself, Will, or their siblings. It's been amazing to witness.

It feels like my husband and I are not on our own raising our kids, the Lord is very much in our midst, and He speaks with them all day long and guides them just as much as He guides us. It's a truly comforting thought.

He knows their giftings, talents, and abilities, and He knows their character traits and their destinies, and He is invested in seeing them know Him intimately and fulfilling their destinies.

The Lord also wants me to share with you that if your children are really young, you don't have to be stressed about finding quiet time with the Lord. You can spend time with Him in the midst of all your little ones. It is good for them to see you spend time with God, to see you worship, and to hear your prayers. You can also invite them to join in. This pleases the Lord very much.

To close, I just want to reiterate that it is not hard to lead your children into encountering God for themselves. You have the Holy Spirit inside of you, Who leads and guides you in all things. He will help you to know how to lead your children into an intimate relationship with their Heavenly Father, and He will show you how to create an environment in your home that is conducive to the presence of God, just like Samuel had when he was raised in the Temple. You will partner with God to raise children whose hearts are perfect towards Him and who fulfill their destinies.

Front Row (Left to right): Dana, Kiera, Lily, Grace, Justin.
Back Row (Left to Right): Jerome, Will, Judah.

About the Author

Dana Bellamy married and started her family at a young age. Wed to a US Marine, she was taken away from everything familiar in her home country of Australia and moved halfway across the world to totally different land. Dana felt like Abraham in Genesis. Yet, the Lord was faithful. He took Dana by the hand and led her on the journey of learning who He is and what His Word really says. He also taught her how to be a godly wife and mother.

Today Dana is a graduate of Charis Bible College Colorado, with a minister's license as well as an Associate's degree in Biblical Studies. She and her husband are in their nineteenth year of marriage and have six precious children. Together, they manage their own flight school "On the Fly Aviation", where the Lord fulfilled Dana's lifelong dream to become a private pilot. Dana's family is known for their happy marriage and for the joy and obedience of their children. Dana regularly encourages wives and mothers on their important God-given assignment and helps them raise their own children to love the Lord and fulfill their God-given destinies.

Other Books Published by Dana Bellamy

Raising Happy Hearts

www.ingramcontent.com/pod-product-compliance
Lightning Source LLC
Chambersburg PA
CBHW071954070426
42453CB00008BA/757